KT-872-706

All words written by Ian McCulloch

Songs published by Warner Chappell Music Publishing Ltd except,
"An Eternity Turns", "Buried Alive", "Burn for Me", "Everybody Knows", "Flowers", "Hide And Seek", "It's Alright", "King Of Kings", "Make Me Shine", "Marble Towers", "Scratch The Past" and "Supermellowman" published by Warner Chappell Music Publishing Ltd./ Universal Music Publishing Ltd. "All Because Of You Day", "Another Train", "Arthur", "Baby Hold On", "Everything Kills You", "High Wires", "In The Margins", "Kansas", "Love In Veins", "Make Us Blind", "Of A Life", "Parthenon Drive", "Playgrounds And Cityparks", "Scissors In The Sand", "She Sings", "Siberia", "Sideways Eight", "Stormy Weather", "Slideling", "Stake Your Claim" and "What If I Were" published by Universal Music Publishing Ltd. "Big Days", "Candleland", "Faith And Healing", "Fear Of The Known", "Horse's Head", "In Bloom", "I Know You Well", "Pots Of Gold", "Pro Patria Mori", "Proud To Fall", "Proxy", "Raindrops On The Sun", "The Cape", "The Dead End", "The Flickering Wall", "The Fountain" "The Idolness Of Gods", "The White Hotel", "The World Is Flat" and "Toad" published by Killing Moon Songs Limited (Kobalt). "Life Of A Thousand Crimes" and "Shroud Of Turin" published by Killing Moon Songs Limited (Kobalt)/Universal Music Publishing Ltd. "Bombers Bay", "Lost & Found", "Over You" and "The Game" published by Killing Moon Songs Limited (Kobalt)/Warner Chappell Music Publishing Ltd. "Do You Know Who I Am', "Drivetime", "Everlasting Neverendless", "Forgotten Fields" and "Think I Need It Too" published by Killing Moon Songs Limited (Kobalt)/Windswept Pacific (London) Ltd., A BMG Chrysalis Company/Nettwork One Music/Dset Music Publishing/Universal Music Publishing Ltd.

Concept and design: Greg Jakobek
Editor: Paul Toogood
Photography: Alex Hurst

Published in the United Kingdom by
The Lyric Book Company Ltd.
PO Box 796
Godalming
GU7 9GB

First Edition
ISBN 978-0-9570257-1-4

lyricbook.com

the lyrics

of

IAN McCULLOCH

The Lyric Book Company Ltd.

CONTENTS

A PROMISE

You said something will change
We were all dressed up
Somewhere to go
No sign of rain
But something will change
You promised

You said nothing will change
We were almost near
Almost far
Down came the rain
But nothing will change
You promised

A promise
A promise
A promise

It's exactly the same
You said
It's always the same
But I'll make it change
Into something the same
I promise

A promise
A promise
A promise

Light on the waves
Light on the waves
Light on the waves
Light on the waves
A promise, a promise
A promise, a promise
(light on the water)
(we could sail on forever) a promise...

from the album 'Heaven Up Here' 30/5/1981

ALL BECAUSE OF YOU DAYS

I don't want to run
I don't want to hide
I just want to kiss goodnight
Say goodnight one more time

Nothing gets you up
Nothing gets you high
Everything just comes to this
Final mistaken ride

And it's goodbye, goodbye all my new days
Goodbye, all because of you days
Goodbye

You just can't get out
You just can't get in
Everything just has strung you up, hung you up
To watch you swing

One of us is you
And one of us is me
Broken frozen equal parts
Broken hearts breaking free

And it's goodbye, goodbye all my new days
Goodbye, all those chosen few days
Goodbye

Baby maybe someday
Maybe one day
We'll say hi

I don't want to run
I don't want to hide
I just want to kiss goodnight
Say goodnight one last time

Nothing gets you up
Nothing gets me high
Everything just comes to this
Final mistaken ride
One last time

It's goodbye, goodbye all my new days
Goodbye, all because of you days
Goodbye

And it's goodbye, goodbye all my new days
Goodbye, all those chosen few days
New days

Baby maybe someday
Maybe one day
We'll say hi
Baby maybe sometime
Maybe next time
We'll say hi
Baby maybe someday
Maybe one day
We'll say hi
Baby maybe sometime
Maybe next time
We'll say hi

Baby maybe sometime
Maybe next time
We'll say hi
We'll say hi
We'll say hi

Baby maybe someday
Maybe one day
We'll say hi

from the album 'Siberia' 20/9/2005

ALL I WANT

I began to feel so bare
Waking up laughing so rare
Up and down and down the stairs
Sat myself up in the chair

And said all I love is all I love
All I want is all I want

If we make the same mistake
Who could we blame
When we make the same mistake
Who will we blame
Who will we blame
What will we blame?

We'll blame all I love
All I love
All we want
All we want

I had a healthy discussion
I had a sleep in the chair
I lay my head on a cushion
Because it was there
I had a flail in the dark
It was chasing my tail
It was worse than it's bark
It was biting my nails
Up and down and down the stairs
Set myself up in the chair

And said all I love is
All I love
All I want
Is all I want
(You've got the hands)

All I love
(To hold the key)
Is all I love
All I want
(You've got the hands)
Is all I want
(To hold the key)

If we make the same mistakes
Who could we blame?
When we make the same mistake
Who could we blame?
Who will we blame
What could we blame?
When we make
The same mistake
Who will we blame?...

from the album 'Heaven Up Here' 30/5/1981

ALL IN YOUR MIND

You say your proud to be
One of the people
Hands on the money
And your feet on the ground
Shouting out loud
From the top of the steeple
Counting the flock while
Collecting their pounds
All you thieving wheeler dealers
In the healing zone
Giving me fever fever fever fever
Down to my bones

I pray
And nothing happens
Jesus it's all in my mind
You say
Stop looking for answers
And reasons
They're all in your mind
All in you mind

Covered in flies
And smothered in lava
I can't scratch my itches
With these pumice stone hands
I dream of my days
As a desert farmer
Living my life
On the fat of the sand
All you thieving wheeler dealers
In the healing zone
Giving me fever fever fever fever
Down to my bones

I pray
And nothing happens
Jesus it's all in my mind
You say
Stop looking for answers
And reasons
They're all in your mind
All in your mind

Stuck in a world
Losing its way and wonder
I wonder what happened
To the world we knew
Splitting the atom
And feeling its thunder
Could never ever make me
Feel the way you do
You give me fever fever fever fever
Down to my bones
Fever fever fever fever
In the healing zone

I pray
And nothing happens
Jesus it's all in my mind
You say
Stop looking for answers
And reasons
They're all in your mind
All in your mind

from the album 'Echo & The Bunnymen' 6/7/1987

ALL MY COLOURS (ZIMBO)

Flying
And you know I'm not coming down
You're trying
But you know you must soon go down
All my colours
Turn to clouds
All my colours
Turn to cloud

Zimbo zimbo zimbo zimbo zimbo
Zimbo zimbo zimbo zimbo zimbo
Zimbo zimbo zimbo zimbo zimbo
Zimbo zimbo zimbo zimbo zimbo

What d'you say
When your heart's in pieces?
How d'you play
Those cards in sequence?
That box you gave me
Burned nicely
That box you gave me
Burned nicely

Zimbo zimbo zimbo zimbo zimbo
Zimbo zimbo zimbo zimbo zimbo
Zimbo zimbo zimbo zimbo zimbo
Zimbo zimbo zimbo zimbo zimbo

Flying down
Flying down

All my colours
Turn to clouds
All my colours
Turn to cloud

Hey I've flown away
Hey I've flown away
That box you gave me
Burned nicely
That box you gave me
Burned nicely
Hey I've flown away
Hey I've flown away
All my colours

from the album 'Heaven Up Here' 30/5/1981

ALL THAT JAZZ

Where the hell have you been?
We've been waiting with our best suits on
Hair slicked back and all that jazz
Rolling down the Union Jack
See you at the barricades babe
See you when the lights go low, Joe
Hear you when the wheels turn round
Someday when the sky turns black

It appeals because it's what I feel
I know I don't understand
If you ask you know I don't mind kneeling
But when my knees hurt I like to stand
Instinct is the common law y'all
A million years won't erase
Strike that chord I'm searching for
Call it a committed race

No matter how I shake my fist
I know I can't resist it
No matter how you shake your fist
You know you can't resist it
See you at the barricades babe
See you when the lights go low, Joe
Hear you when the wheels turn round
Someday when the sky turns black

from the album 'Crocodiles' 18/7/1980

ALTAMONT

Hey now love, I'm right in the middle of
A hurricane that's blown my way
God's above and all he's really thinking of is
How much pain you've gotta pay

Why do you do it?
'Cos it does for you
Why do I do it?
'Cos it does me, too
Don't mind if I do
No I don't mind if I do
Yeah, yeah...

Hey now, love why are you so scared of
The light that breaks your darkest days
I've done stuff and things you've never heard of
Souls lost along the way

Why do you do it?
'Cos it does for you
Why do I do it?
'Cos it does me, too
Don't mind if I do
No I don't mind if I do
Yeah, yeah...

Hey now, love, what are you made of?
From the clay or to the dust
It isn't love you're afraid of
It's losing faith in all you trust

It's now, my Altamont
It's now, my Altamont
My Altamont...

from the album 'Evergreen' 14/7/1997

AN ETERNITY TURNS

Look Ma, it's me, no hands on the wheel
Nothing can touch you, when you can't even feel
No one you can trust, 'cos no one's for real
No one's for real

Father forget us, or father forgive us
Giving us faith, and then calling us sinners

Mixing up the losers, with all of the winners
Tonight... yeah yeah yeah

  Kneeling at the crossroads
  All my bridges burning
  Down the river my life flows
  Took another wrong turning

Knows what she feels, but he's never felt her
Wanted a home, but he needed a shelter
Never gonna win, with the hand he dealt her

Ace's low... tonight
Yeah yeah yeah

  Kneeling at the crossroads
  All my bridges burning
  Down the river my life flows
  Took another wrong turning

I will find you...

I know you only want to share my pain
But I've got something weird pumping through my veins
Got the type of blood that can't be changed... can't be changed

  Kneeling at the crossroads
  All my bridges burning
  Down the river my life flows
  Took another wrong turning

from the album 'Flowers' 16/2/2001

ANGELS AND DEVILS

Call it a day
When night becomes a mad escape
Forgetting the things you mean to say
When all the right words come too late
And everything falls out of place
Under the pillow
Out of the race
Out of the window

  Devils on my shoulder

So so happy
When happiness spells misery
And mister me
Hoping to be
Where ugliness meets beauty
And if you'll see
The demon in you
The angel in me
The Jesus in you
The devil in me

  Angels on my shoulder

Called it a day
When night became my bad escape
Forgetting the things I meant to say
When all the right words came too late
And everything fell out of place
Under the pillow
Out of the race
Out of the window

  Devils on my shoulder
  Angels coming closer

b side from the single 'Silver' 13/4/1983

ANOTHER TRAIN

Too late, I know, it's time to let it go
Don't wait, you know you've got to let it out, to let it show
And you know that something's coming
The writing's on the wall
The winds of change are starting to blow
I know

  Baby's on another train
  She's gonna make this trip alone
  Baby's on another train
  She's going home, going home, going home

Can't take it slow
'Cos yesterday's today's tomorrow
The stakes seem low
Until you have to pay for what you borrow
'Cos you know that something's coming
The writing's on the wall
The wind of change is starting to blow
I know

  Baby's on another train
  She's gonna make this trip alone
  Baby's on another train
  She's going home, going home, going home

Too late, I know, it's time to let it go
Don't wait, you know you've got to let it out, to let it show
'Cos you know that something's coming
The writing's on the wall
The wind of change is starting to blow
I know

  Baby's on another train
  She's gonna make this trip alone
  Baby's on another train
  She's going home, going home, going home

from the album 'Slideling' 28/4/2003

ARTHUR

Fill the skies with stars of wonder
And don't you cry
I don't like it like that
Fill my dreams with love forever
And I'll believe
I'll believe in all that

 Live and die with me
 Live and die with me
 What I wouldn't give now love?
 What I wouldn't give now
 What I wouldn't give now love?
 What I wouldn't give now, now now

Fill my life with moons and moonlight
And shine up my nights
Yeah, I like it like that

 Live and die with me
 Live and die with me
 What I wouldn't give now love?
 What I wouldn't give now
 What I wouldn't give now love?
 What I wouldn't give now, now now

Fill the skies with stars of wonder
And don't you cry
I don't like it like that
Don't like it like that

from the album 'Slideling' 28/4/2003

BABY HOLD ON

When your life is wrong
And your days are gone
And the Night is coming on
Baby hold on
Baby hold on
Baby hold on

When your race is run
And the prize is won
Make the words to your song
Baby hold on
Baby hold on
Baby hold on

When it feels like no one listens
And it seems like no one hears you call
When your star no longer glistens
I'll be there to catch you
You won't fall
You won't fall

When your day is done
Like a setting sun
And the night keeps coming on
Baby hold on
Baby hold on
Baby hold on
Baby hold on
Baby hold on

from the album 'Slideling' 28/4/2003

BABY RAIN

Lost again
Still waiting for the voices
That don't call my name
Had too many choices
And I missed my aim
No pearls inside the oysters

Just a world
With no answers
We all get life
And take our chances

  In the rain
  Baby rain
  In the rain
  Baby rain

Glad to be
Alive and still believing
What you said to me
Your love was never leaving
And it comes for free
So what's the use of stealing

From your girl?
When she's the answer
And your world?
And your chances?

  In the rain
  Baby rain
  In the rain
  Baby rain

I've got what you want
When're you going to get me?

Home again
I can hear the voices
Singing out my name
Life is where the choice is
And I've found my aim
Don't need pearls or oysters

Just a world
With all the answers
I've got life
I'll take my chances

In the rain
Baby rain
In the rain
Baby Rain

from the album 'What Are You Going To Do With Your Life?' 16/4/1999

BASEBALL BILL

Here I go, it must be four in a row
I've gotta get my head down tonight
But you know I know
When the streets are aglow
I'll be headed for the city of lights

You talkin' to me?
'Cos I don't want to know, no, no, no
You can't even see
What's already on show

I'm hitting my prime and you're wasting my time
You're denominator commonest low
My head's burning up and I'm down on my luck
See you in the 48th row
With a matchbox full and a sulphurous skull
I'm trynna set my mind to rights
I'm gonna burn, burn, burn as the universe turns
Out of mind and out of sight

You talkin' to me?
'Cos I don't want to know, no, no, no
You can't even see
What's already on show

Baseball Bill went in for the kill
He blew it when he found his soul
Lost his will to live when he saw someone give
'Cos giving always takes its toll

You talkin' to me?
'Cos I don't want to know, no, no, no
You can't even see
What's already on show

Ooh, Baseball Bill...

from the album 'Evergreen' 14/7/1997

BEDBUGS & BALLYHOO

Buffalo and bison
Bison and buffalo
Cannonball and rifle
Rifle and Cannonball
That's the way the thunder rumbles
That's the way the thunder rumbles
Rumbles...

 Down on your knees again
 Saying please again yeah yeah yeah

Kangaroo and chipmunk
Chipmunk and kangaroo
Ballyhoo and bedbugs
Bedbugs and ballyhoo
That's the way the bee bumbles
That's the way the bee bumbles
That's the way the bee bumbles
That's the way the bee bumbles
Bumbles...

 Down on your kness again
 Saying please again no no no
 No

 Down on your knees again
 Saying please again
 Down on you knees again
 Saying please again no no no

Buffalo and bison
Bison and buffalo
Cannonball and rifle
Rifle and Cannonball
That's the way the thunder rumbles
That's the way the thunder rumbles
That's the way the thunder rumbles
That's the way the thunder rumbles
Rumbles rumbles rumbles

from the album 'Echo & The Bunnymen' 6/7/1987

BIG DAYS

There I was
Read the news out of a comic
D'you remember us?
We had dreams just like those rockets
That were heading for the moon
They were heading for the moon

  Home is where the house is
  House where the toys stay
  The sky always blue
  With the noises of big days

In true low
I was hotter than the others
In a world below
They were floating down the gutters
And the tide was coming in
And the tide was coming in

  Home is where the house is
  House where the toys stay
  The sky always blue
  With the noises of big days

Big days
All my big days...
All mine

b side from the single 'Candleland (The Second Coming)' 1/1/1990

BOMBERS BAY

The word went round
in no dream town
They shut us up
and the shutters down
The planes flew in
and laid the ground
We built upon
and spun around
God's one miracle
Lost in circles

On the march
Berlin to Bombers Bay
Traveling dark
on the road to Mandalay

Cannon fire
came to call
Stood us up
and watched us fall
The way we were
and now outworn
Our costumes changed
to uniforms
Black black days
here to stay

On the march
Madrid to Bombers Bay
Traveling dark
on the road to Mandalay

Pack up your troubles and you'll all get by
Smile boys that's the style
Pack up your troubles and you'll all get by
Smile

They give us hope
and teach us well
with magic moons
that cast a spell
and hypnotise
and draw us in
I believe
I'm believing
God's one miracle
moves in circles

On the march
Berlin to Bombers Bay
Traveling dark
on the road

On the march
Berlin to Bombers Bay
Traveling dark
on the roads to Mandalay

Black black days
where the flying fishes play
Black black days
where the flying fishes play
Black black days
where the flying fishes play
Black black days
where the flying fishes play...

from the album 'Echo & The Bunnymen' 6/7/1987

BRING ON THE DANCING HORSES

Jimmy Brown
Made of stone
Charlie Clown
No way home

Bring on the dancing horses
Headless and all alone
Shiver and say the words
Of every lie you've heard

First I'm gonna make it
Then I'm gonna break it
'Til it falls apart
Hating all the faking
And shaking while I'm breaking
Your brittle heart

Billy stands
All alone
Sinking sand
Skin and bone

Bring on the dancing horses
Wherever they may roam
Shiver and say the words
Of every lie you've heard

First I'm gonna make it
Then I'm gonna break it
'Til it falls apart
Hating all the faking
And shaking while I'm breaking
Your brittle heart
Brittle heart...
And my little heart goes...

Jimmy Brown
Made of stone
Charlie clown
No way home

Bring on the headless horses
Wherever they may roam
Shiver and say the words
Of every lie you've heard

First I'm gonna make it
Then I'm gonna break it
'Til it falls apart
Hating all the faking
And shaking while you're breaking
My brittle heart
Brittle heart...
And our little hearts go...

Bring on the new messiah
Wherever he may roam
Bring on the new messiah
Wherever he may roam
First I'm gonna break him
Then I'm gonna make him
Find his own way home

from the album 'Songs To Learn And Sing' 15/11/1985

BROKE MY NECK

I forget
Just what I meant
Broke my neck
Lost Respect
It was my fall from grace
I'm dead was
What I meant
Lost all track
And away I went
No sign of face to face
No chance of face to face

I helped myself
I couldn't help myself
I tell myself
Go on and help yourself
You can help yourself
I can help myself

No sign of face to face...

b side of the single 'A Promise' 10/7/1981

BURIED ALIVE

Buried alive
Person unknown
Dying inside
Half the way home
Somewhere under a Delvaux moon
Our childhoods end came too soon
Came too soon

Don't want to know when
Don't wanna know why
Don't wanna believe that life is just to die
You were the one who sang lullabies
I'm still hanging out to dry, out to dry

Hey now, hey now
Don't you cry
It's just the dying of the light
Time to say our goodbyes
I'll look for you in that goodnight

Is anybody here ?
I wanna go out, the way I came in
My flame blowing out
In the summer wind
And some where under a Delvaux moon
Childhoods end came too soon
Came too soon

Hey now, hey now
Don't you cry
It's just the dying of the light
Time to say our goodbyes
I'll look for you in that goodnight

Goodnight
Goodnight
Goodnight

from the album 'Flowers' 16/2/2001

BURNED

Looking for a taste of the honey
I'm wondering if it ever comes
You said when it comes to the honey
You gotta give it 'til you get some

You look like you got the answers
All I got's a handful of clues
It's too late for choice and reason
Let's do it like the chosen few

All you gotta do for me
Is open up and turn it on
All you gotta do for me
Is open up and turn it on

Closing all the doors of deception
I'm out in the dirty air
I know there's only one direction
I'm gonna live it 'til I get there

You look like you got the answers
All I got's a handful of clues
It's too late for choice and reason
Let's do it like the chosen few

All you gotta do for me
Is open up and turn me on
All you gotta do for me
Is open up and turn it on

Turn turn turn it on...

from the album 'Burned' 1/10/1995

BURN FOR ME

I'm water... swim to me
Be my fire... burn with me

One day, you'll see
After the fall has fallen
One day, I'll be
The one you're heart's still calling

I'm air... breathe with me
Be my prayer... believe in me

One night, you'll see
The moon and stars in motion
One night, your sea
Will melt in to my ocean

I'm water... swim to me
Be my fire... burn for me

I'm going out...

One day, you'll see
After the fall has fallen
One day, I'll be
The one you're heart's still calling

One night, you'll see
The moon and stars in motion
One night, your sea
Will melt in to my ocean

from the album 'Flowers' 16/2/2001

CANDLELAND

Get your handful of remembrance
For you to sprinkle through your life
In between the penance
That you carry by your side
With the make-belief and miracles
That only come alive

In Candleland
Candleland

Wear your guilt like skin
And keep your sins disguised
Take some salt and sugar
And rub it in your eyes
You'll know that something's left you
Just as you arrive

In Candleland
Candleland

I walked back inside me
I'd gone back for my youth
As I came down the fire escape
It must have stayed up on the roof
They say you just know
And that knowing is the proof

Of Candleland
Candleland...

from the album 'Candleland' 17/9/1989

CLAY

Am I the half of half-and-half
Or am I the half that's whole?
I've got to be one with all my halves
It's my worthy earthly goal
It's my worthy earthly goal
It's my worthy earthly goal

Are you the heavy half
Of the lighter me?
Are you the ready part
Of the rightful me?

When I came apart
I wasn't made of sand
When you fell apart
Clay crumbled in my hands
Along with a life load
Of statues and haloes

Am I the half of half-and-half?
Or am I the half that's whole?
Am I the half that's whole?
Am I the half that's whole?

Are you the wrongful half
Of the rightful me?
Are you the mongol half
Of the cerebral me?

When I came apart
I wasn't made of sand
When you fell apart
Clay crumbled in my hands
When I came apart
I wasn't made of sand
When you fell apart
Clay crumbled in my hands

If we exercise just some control
When we exercise our sum control

Oh isn't it nice
When your heart is made out of ice
Oh isn't it nice
When your heart is made out of ice

Are you the heavy half
Of the lighter me
Are you the ready part
of the hesitant me

Am I the "shall" in po-ten-tial
Or am I the "suck" in "cess"
Pools of delusion
Deluge me
Am I the more or less
Am I the more or less
Am I the more or less

When I came apart
I wasn't made of sand
When you fell apart
Clay crumbled in my hands
When I came apart
I wasn't made of sand

When I was the Cain
You were the Abel
When I came apart
Clay crumbled in my hands

from the album 'Porcupine' 4/2/1983

CLOSE YOUR EYES

Nip it in the bud
I'd do it if I could
Do it if I could
Always knew I should and
Never understood
Never understood

I will go where I must
Taking in what I can
I will go if I must
Making up what I can

  Close your eyes
  (Yeah yeah yeah)...
  Close your eyes
  (Yeah yeah yeah)...
  Look inside
  Look inside

Another eyeball pain and
Vision down the drain
Going down the drain
And all my yester know days
Will never be the same
Never be the same

I will go if I must
Taking in what I can
I will go 'cos I must
Making up what I can

  Close your eyes
  (I'm trying to)
  Close your eyes
  (I'm going to)...
  Close your eyes
  (I'm trying to)

Close your eyes
(I'm going to)...
Look inside...
Look inside...

My destiny
I know will be
The best that mine
Ever can be

There's no use lying
I'm just as scared of dying as everyone
Someone in the know said
You're a long time dead
He's never wrong

Close your eyes
(I'm trying to)
Close your eyes
(I'm going to)...
Close your eyes
(I'm trying to)
Close your eyes
(I'm going to)...
Look inside...
Look inside...

Is there something in your mind?
Are you slipping on a stone?
If there's nothing in your mind
Won't you leave my world alone?
Leave my world
Leave my world
Alone

from the album 'Mysterio' 17/3/1992

CROCODILES

I read it in a magazine
I don't wanna see it again
I threw away the magazine
And looked for someone to explain
I don't wanna look back
I can't look around
I don't wanna see it coming round

Listen to the ups and downs
Listen to the sound they make
Don't be scared when it gets loud
When you're skin begins to shake
'Cause you don't wanna look back
You gotta look tall
You gotta see those creeps crawl

I know you know
I know you know

I can see you've got the blues
In your alligator shoes
Me, I'm all smiles
I got my crocodiles
I don't wanna look back
I can't turn around
I don't want to see it coming down

Met someone just the other day
Said wait until tomorrow
I said, hey what you doing today
He said, I'm going to do it tomorrow
Met someone just the other day
Said wait until tomorrow
I said, hey, what you doing today
I'm going to do it tomorrow

from the album 'Crocodiles' 18/7/1980

CRYSTAL DAYS

Here am I
Whole at last with a golden view
Looking for hope
And I hope it's you
Splitting my heart
Cracked right in two
The pleasure of pain endured

To purify our misfit ways
And magnify our crystal days

Where are you
In shadows only I can see
Looking for hope
And you hope it's me
Tattered and torn and born to be
Building a world where we can

Purify our misfit ways
And magnify our crystal days

Pure and to magnify

Here am I
Whole at last with a golden view
Looking for hope
And I know it's you
Splitting my heart
Cracked right in two

The pleasure of pain enjoyed
To purify our misfit ways
And magnify our crystal days
Purify our misfit ways
And magnify our crystal days

Doo da doo doo doo da doo
Doo da doo doo doo da doo
Doo da doo doo doo da doo
Doo da doo doo doo da doo

Days

from the album 'Ocean Rain' 8/5/1984

DAMNATION

Got my suit of armour on
Trynna find some kind of meaning
A peg to hang a hope upon
Something real to stop me dreaming
I'm thinking
I'm thinking
And thinking starts me feeling

  Damn damnation
  Damn damn nation
  Damn damnation
  Damn damn nation

Snowflakes on the oven top
Drumbeats in the wild blue yonder
Didn't hear the penny drop
Shenendoah I'm doomed to wander
I'm hoping
I'm hoping
No more no longer

  Damn damnation
  Damn damn nation
  Damn damnation
  Damn damn nation

Got my ticket to the game
Bullets in a darkened chamber
Every one a different frame
Each an old familiar danger
I'm changing
I'm changing
No more the stranger

  Damn damnation, damn damn nation
  Damn damnation, damn damn nation
  Damn damn
  Nation

from the album 'Mysterio' 17/3/1992

DO IT CLEAN

I've got a handful of this
What do I do with it?
I've got a barrel of this
What do I do with it?
I do it clean, I do it clean

  Do it clean, do it clean
  Know what I mean
  Do it clean, do it clean
  I know what I mean, I mean

Where am I going?
Where have I been?
Where are you going?
Where have you been?
I've been here, I've been there

I've been here, there, everywhere
Here there nowhere
Iszy bitzy witzy itzy everywhere
I've been here and I've been there
I've been

I had a handful of this
What did I do with it?
I had a barrel of this
What did I do with it?
I did it clean, I did it clean

Do it clean, do it clean
Know what I mean?
Do it clean, do it clean
I know what I mean

from the album 'Crocodiles' 18/7/1980

DO YOU KNOW WHO I AM?

Love it, hate it
Want it, had it
Need it, got it
Down-da-down-da-down

Take it, took it
Shaked it, shooked it
Flaked it, flucked it
Down-da-down-da-down...

 Do you know who I am?
 Do you know what I've got?
 Do you know who I am?
 'Cause I know what you're not

Read it, wrote it
Heard it, spoked it
Made it, broked it
Down-da-down-da-down

 Do you know who I am?
 Do you know what I've got?
 Do you know who I am?
 'Cause I know what you're not

Love it, hate it
Want it, had it
Need it, got it
Down-da-down-da-down

 Do you know who I am?
 Do you know what I've got?
 Do you know who I am?
 'Cause I know what you're not

from the album 'The Fountain' 12/10/2009

DON'T LET IT GET YOU DOWN

You were really something else
Made me forget myself
My lights came on
When I got to you
You were almost through
Yeah, almost gone

  Don't let it get you down
  Don't let it get you down
  When the moon and the stars go crashing 'round
  Don't let it get you down

An angel walked amongst us
Tried but couldn't love us
Something's wrong
Since you've gone
You know there's nothing and no-one
To hang love on

So tell me how it feels
Tell me how it feels
To touch the flame
Tell me who I am
Tell me who I really am
What's my name?

  Don't let it get you down
  Don't let it get you down
  When the moon and the stars go crashing 'round
  Don't let it get you down

God's above us
And Jesus loves us
Yeah, God's above us
And Jesus loves us

If you want it, you can get it
If you want it, you can get it
If you want it, come and get it
Right now

from the album 'Evergreen' 14/7/1997

DRIVETIME

If we ride ride ride
Rider come on to the other side
Floating and floating on the night tide
Just beyond where the sun dies

If we fly fly fly
Fly with me now over oceans wide
Higher than heaven, higher than the sky
You, me and God can watch the sun rise

Drivetime
On the drivetime
Driving by

If we ride ride ride
Where the mist takes us
In a rising tide
Makes us and breaks us there's no-one to guide
Spirits following the blind

If we fly fly fly
Will it take us up too high-high
A prayer and no wings just a why why?
We can't see the skyline for the sky

Drivetime
On the drivetime
Driving by

from the album 'The Fountain' 12/10/2009

DUG FOR LOVE

Lost horizons and tomorrows
Disappeared along the way
Led me on and on
I followed up
Got sent to yesterday
Leaves are falling down from Heaven
Autumn in the auburn skies
One and one and five is seven
One and one and three is five

  All my love
  Buried it deep and you dug it up
  All my love
  Buried it deep and you dug it up

Destination: life and living
Use the privilege of birth
All you need is all you know is
All you'll get is all you're worth
Dot-to-dot I'll take what's given
Golden apples of the sun
Forbid
For bitten
Ending what's just begun
Just begun...

  All my love
  Buried it deep and you dug it up
  All my love
  Buried it deep and you dug it up
  All your love
  Buried it deep and you dug it up

All my love
All your love...

Looking for the piece to put me together
Link the link, link the chain
Time for the priest, for the man for all weather
Never ever ever gonna think it again
Leave me all the scrapings from the dregs of Heaven
Just don't leave me waiting at the gates of hell
Only wanna go where the great are heading
Between the falling and the fully felled

All my love
Buried it deep and you dug it up...
All my love
All your love...

from the album 'Mysterio' 17/3/1992

EMPIRE STATE HALO

Gazed in the crystal ball
Looks like I'm lost again
Where do I find the tunnel's end?
Followed the rise and fall
Of all the better men
From here to Bethlehem

 All free souls beware
 The moon is in my hair

Around the Empire State
I saw the angels fly
Heaven above and ten below
We don't have long to wait
Ran out of alibis
Ran out of things I'll ever know

The streets were paved with gold
And I saw your halo glow

And this love is just for you
And your love will learn to love me, too
Love me, too

 All free souls beware
 The moon is in my hair

And this love is just for you
And your love will learn to love me, too
Love me, too

The moon is in my hair

from the album 'Evergreen' 14/7/1997

EVERGREEN

There's no more wishes in the well
No more dreams to sell
No time in the hourglass
There's no more lies for you to tell
Your Heaven is your hell
Your future dying in the past

Evergreen
Ever, ever, evergreen
Evergreen

I know I'm never gonna learn
Fingers fit to burn
You can't let the fire die
Keep the flames of your desire
Always rising higher
Aim for stars and hit the sky

Evergreen
Ever, ever, evergreen
Evergreen

from the album 'Evergreen' 14/7/1997

EVERLASTING NEVERENDLESS

Everlasting neverendless
Moments lost in time
Every last thing they can send us
Will be yours and mine

Don't look down...

 See this through or we could watch it die
 Me and you, saying our last goodbye
 Baby why?

Hear us calling
Ever crying
Wonder when it stops

Don't look down...

 See this through or we could watch it die
 Me and you, saying our last goodbye
 Baby why ?

See this through...

from the album 'The Fountain' 12/10/2009

EVERYBODY KNOWS

Everybody knows, how your garden grows
Everybody knows, how your garden grows
Everyone can see, I'm blind as blind can be
The woods look just like trees
Look like trees to me

And I don't even get it
I don't know what you're trying to say
You're never gonna let me forget it
It's always gonna get in the way

It's moving much too fast
You know it ain't gonna last
I think we're heading for a crash
Heading for a crash

It's coming to a natural end
I'm going round my last bend
There's some things you just can't mend
Things you just can't mend

I can't even remember
I don't know what the day is today
You're putting the No in November
And taking all the bes out of May

Everybody knows, how your garden grows
Everybody knows, how your garden grows
Everyone can see, I'm blind as blind can be
The woods look just like trees
Look like trees to me

And I don't even get it
I don't know what you're trying to say
You're never gonna let me forget it
It's always gonna get in the way

from the album 'Flowers' 16/2/2001

EVERYTHING KILLS YOU

And when it comes
Always too late
You put the future behind you

Then when it's gone
Always too soon
You put the past in front of you, in front of you

Everything takes you
Everything aches you
Everything breaks you
Everything spills you
Everything ills you
Everything kills you

And when the world
Is never enough
Nothing at all's too much for you

And when what's real
Is always too tough
Nothing at all can touch you, touch you

Everything takes you
Everything fakes you
Everything breaks you
Everything wills you
Everything chills you
Everything kills you

And when your heart's in pieces
And when your heart's in pieces
It's when the world's in pieces now
The world's in pieces now
The world's in pieces now

And when it comes
Always too late
You've got the future behind you

Then when it's gone
Always too soon
You've put the past in front of you, in front of you

Everything takes you
Everything aches you
Everything breaks you
Everything spills you
Everything ills you
Everything kills you
Everything takes you
Everything makes you
Everything fakes you
Everything wills you
Everything chills you
Everything kills you
Everything kills you
Everything kills you

Everyone kills you
Everyone kills you
Everything kills you

from the album 'Siberia' 20/9/2005

FAITH & HEALING

Everyone was running scared
Someone talked and someone heard
The twisted end to all the words
That I'd hung on to
One more time inside the dream
Where nothing has to be this real
And I don't ever have to feel
What I don't want to

You once said I thought too much
But never thought enough to touch
Eyes so sad
Evergreen
The saddest eyes I've ever seen

Lost all reason and belonging
Can't do right for doing wrong and
I don't like the way I'm feeling
Need your faith and healing healing healing
Faith and healing...

Pick me up and hold me there
Leave me hanging in the air
'Til I promise I will care
The way I used to
Diamonds in the pool tonight
Reminds me of what nights were like
Before I fell into a life
That I got used to

The shining sea, the silver sky
A perfect world before my eyes
Don't be scared, don't you cry
If all the world goes passing by

Lost all reason and belonging
Can't do right for doing wrong and
I don't like the way I'm feeling
Need your faith, faith and healing
Faith and healing...

You once said I thought too much
But never thought enough to touch

from the album 'Candleland' 17/9/1989

FEAR OF THE KNOWN

When the night descends because of you
And the darkness is your point of view
Loneliness belongs only to you
Nothing is the only thing to do

Fear of the known
Walking the pavement

When the road's a voyage you can't make
And the role's a part you've had to fake
When godliness has sucked away your hope
And hopelessness is hanging by a rope

When will it happen?
How does it end?
Never to happen
Ever again

Fear of the known
Walking the pavement
Fear of the known
Slipping and sliding

Loneliness belongs only to you
Nothing is the only thing to do

When will it happen?
How does it end?
Never to happen
Ever again

b side from the single 'Faith & Healing' 28/2/1990

FLOWERS

I've been laying down the flowers
I've been waiting in the sun
I've been counting down the hours
One by one
One by one

I've been catching my reflection
I'm still looking at someone
Still perfecting imperfection
Like everyone
Every no one

I even saw it come
Knew the hit would run and run
And I, as it came undone
Knew that I'd lost everything
Everything I'd won

Here's to all the things we'll never
Here's to all we could have done
Here's to what became whatever
Whatever web we spun, web we spun

I even saw it come
Knew the hit would run and run
And I, as it came undone
Knew that I'd lost everything
Everything I'd won

I've been laying down the flowers
I've been waiting in the sun
I've been counting down the hours
One by one
One by one

from the album 'Flowers' 16/2/2001

FOOLS LIKE US

It's fools like us
Always fooled
By the bright side of life
Then life on the cool
How does it turn
How does it turn
Into dying embers
From a love that burned?

On its way to your heart somehow...

They're falling again
My shining stars
From out of your Heaven
And into my heart
Ribbons and chains
Ribbons and chains
Tie us together
And keep us apart

Got to get to your heart somehow...

If I could be someone
Someone better than me
I would be that someone
Who's still waiting to be free

It's fools like us
Always burned
On the dying embers
Of a love that turned

On its way to your heart somehow...

Gotta get to your heart somehow
Gotta get to your heart somehow
Gotta get to your heart somehow

Time is on our side...

from the album 'What Are You Going To Do With Your Life?' 16/4/1999

FORGIVEN

I'm just one of many
Who gave a love in vain
Sold it out for pennies
And saved up all my rain

What d'you want from me?
The ocean or the sea?
The salt inside the rising tide
Of tears you got from me
Got from me
Got from me, yeah...

One day I'll be ready
To take what could be mine
And everything I've buried
I'll lay out on the line

What d'you want to see?
The truth or mystery?
A blinding light? Or blackest night?
They're both inside of me
Inside me
Inside me, yeah...

I'm just one of many
Who took a love in vain
Sold it out for pennies
And saved up all my rain

What d'you want from me
The truth or mystery?
The salt inside the rising tide
Of tears you got from me
Got from me
Got from me, yeah

I don't want to be forgiven
All I want is to be free
I know I'll never be forgiven
I know I'll never be free

from the album 'Evergreen' 14/7/1997

FORGOTTEN FIELDS

In the tree-lined cities and forgotten fields
Some are born too pretty, some are born too real
Some to death-wish pity, while the selfish steal some ground

It's all just hunchbacked plans too stumped to feel
As the rise of man names his price to deal
It's "look ma, no hands" on the steering wheel, going round
Goes round, goes round, goes round, slows down

Some are early bloom, some are made to wait
Some arrive too soon, some leave too late
Some think the moon can navigate their life round
Life round, life round, life round, lives round

Hey... can't you see?
What will be...
Can't you see?

It's behind you
Look behind you

Hey... can't you see?
What will be...
Can't you see?

from the album 'The Fountain' 12/10/2009

FUEL

There is an easier route

Have you had enough
Of your infancy, well?
Would you pass me the bit
Between Heaven and hell?
There's an easier route
The hypotenuse
By bypassing the tongue
Home and dry and unstuck

 Come and get me
 I'm coming ready or not
 I can teach you
 A few minor things
 A hymn to learn and sing

Falling over ourselves
Never bothered to choose
Do they laugh at your need?
Are they changing to you?

There's a book on the floor
Many pages for me
I can fit it too well
Do you know what that means?

 Come and get me
 I'm coming ready or not
 Falling over myself
 Getting ahead of you...

Have you had enough
Of your infancy, well?
Are you planning the move
Between Heaven and Hell?

You can teach me
A few major things
Some animal things
Some hymns to learn and sing

Come and get me
I'm coming ready or not.....

b side from the single 'The Back Of Love' 14/1/1983

GET IN THE CAR

Let's go and take a starlit drive
To where the shaping of our lives
Had just begun
When we were young
When everything was coming right
In all our dreams of love and life
And we would run
Into the sun

Get in the car
We're taking a ride
We're looking for stars
Looking for satellites
Of love
Of love

Changes coming changes gone
We just want to be someone
Behind the tears
Behind the tears
Nights and days go on and on
And things are coming out all wrong
And no one hears
No one hears

Get in the car
We're taking a ride
We're looking for stars
We're looking for satellites
Get in the car
We're taking a ride
You'll be the star
I'll be your satellite
Of love
Of love

Let's go and take a ride
To all those starry nights
We used to fly upon
When we were young
When everything was coming right
In all our dreams of love and life
And we would run
Into the sun

Nothing's gonna get me down...

from the album 'What Are You Going To Do With Your Life?' 16/4/1999

GODS WILL BE GODS

How can you pretend
When there's so much at stake
That it's a different world
And your hands don't shake?

At the end of the room
In front of the bar
We knew that soon
We'd be making our mark

Why do you defend
The part you have to take
With your fingers on the world
Hoping your hands don't shake?

When you get the time
Why not think about
Connecting yours and mine
And turning in to out?

Back to the bar
I was feeling it
The hole in the floor
Was where I would sit

Positions will be lost
Things will fall in place
The falling will not stop
'Til we have found our face

Oh will you mention
My name
To one
Oh, will you mention
My name
To me

Gods will be gods but my one forgot I was made out of skin
And bones will be bones
but when I came home there was no-one in
So where were you staying
While I was out praying?
Was nobody laying
The foundations?
The fulfilling
Of our killing

How can you pretend
That there's so much at stake
When it's a different world
And everything shakes?

Shake baby shake
Roll baby roll
Gonna hit the highest heights and
Never be told to
Roll baby roll
Shake baby shake
Gonna hit the highest heights and
Make a mistake

from the album 'Porcupine' 4/2/1983

GOING UP

Ain't thou watching my film
Analysing me
Rusty chalkdust walker
Checking up to see
If we should pull
The plugs out, on all the history
And all the mystery

Yeah
The things that shouldn't be
The things that couldn't be
No, things that had to be

Don't you see?
Don't you see?

It's going up up up
It's going up
It's going up up up
It's going up

Let's get the hell out of here
Let's get the hell out of here
Going up
Going down

D'you want to know what's wrong with the world?
Everywhere there's people with no flowers in their hair
Flowers in their hair
Flowers

from the album 'Crocodiles' 18/7/1980

HEADS WILL ROLL

Partly politic
Heads will roll
Mostly politic
God must call
'Till the winning hand does belong to me

What if no one's calling
God then must be falling

If I ever met you
In a private place
I would stare you
You into the ground
That's how I'd articulate
The value of my face
The value of one face

What if no one's calling
God then must be falling
What if no one's calling
God then must be falling
What if no one's calling
God then must be falling
What if no one's calling
God then must be falling

from the album 'Porcupine' 4/2/1983

HEAVEN UP HERE

Where are you now
We're over here
We've got those empty pockets
And we can't afford the beer
We're smoking holes and we've got only dreams
And we're so damn drunk we can't see to steer

 The apple cart upset my head's little brain
 They say the moon in the sky upset my head's little brain

I saw it yippee, I did, I swear
Walking through the hallway
Crawling up the stairs
Abebe baby baby baby Bekila
Given up on whisky
Taken up with tequila

 I'm on my own in my blind alley
 I turn myself around
 So it's swallowing me

Wah chi keeta
Wah chi keeta

Groovy groovy people
We're all groovy groovy people
Groovy groovy people
We're all groovy groovy people
Groovy groovy people
Groovy groovy people

I wonder why, sckronk shonkflay mow de wow
Eel Fromp go Arrhh sniggle flink oschee whaarr
Me and the wall
We're okay, we're okay

F-F-Faustus you've got nothing to fear
It may be hell down there
'Cause it's heaven up here
I'd have given forever for a few good years
But too much of a muchness is too much you hear

The hammer on my chest was an abominable pain
The anvil on my belly was an abdominal strain

Gonna take the bottle
Go take the bottle
Go take a sip

from the album 'Heaven Up Here' 30/5/1981

HEAVEN'S GATE

All the holes in my head are the holes I made
Deep and deeper
Holding me holding me hold
Afraid
Weak and weaker
Will you deliver me?
And turn me into someone
That I want to be?

'Cos all I want to do
All I want to do
All I want to do is be a part of you

  Take love as you find it
  You'll lose your love breaking underneath the waves
  Give love like you take it
  You'll find your love hanging 'round Heaven's gate
  Heaven's gate

I'm taking what's rightfully mine
By birth
Not given to you
My skin and what's left of my mind
Less worth
Are going with me, too
Going with me, too
They're going with me, too
Going with me, too

  Take love as you find it
  You'll lose your love breaking underneath the waves
  Give love as you take it
  You'll find your love hanging 'round Heaven's gate

Hanging 'round Heaven's gate
Hanging 'round Heaven's gate

Is it true what I heard you say
There's nothing going right in your world today?
The glitter and the gold never come your way
Your starbound ride is still delayed

Coming out
Spinning round
Let you in and
Let you down

Take love as you find it
You'll lose your love breaking underneath the waves
Give love as you take it
You'll find your love hanging 'round Heaven's gate

Hanging 'round Heaven's gate
Hanging 'round Heaven's gate

from the album 'Mysterio' 17/3/1992

HIGH WIRES

I'm still trippin' on high wires
My mind is frozen, but my soul's on fire
I'm still wishing on the stars above
Just to give me what I'm dreaming of

To be found, to be found, to be found
Going down, going down, going down
To be found, to be found, to be found

With some kinda love; it's working me over
With some kinda love; it's working me out
With some kinda love; it comes out of nowhere
With some kinda love; you know what I'm talking about

Can't feel the way I should
Never ever thought I'd feel that good
No direction and no way in
Playing games I knew I'd never win
Going down, going down, going down
To be found, to be found, to be found

It's some kinda love; it's working me over
It's some kinda love; it's working me out
It's some kinda love; it comes out of nowhere
It's some kinda love; you know what I'm talking about

from the album 'Slideling' 28/4/2003

HIGHER HELL

Smack in the middle of today
Got to learn new words
Merely got to simply say
I think we all misheard

Cracked in the middle of me
Have to find my heart
Smiling equates with happy
But I know they're miles apart

Just like my lower heaven
You know so well my higher hell

When confronted by
Continuing the course
Will you open up
Or do I have to force
The words right out
Of your stubborn mouth?
Stunted of course,
Guilty in their growth

Just like my lower heaven
You know so well my higher hell

Crashed through the floor today
I couldn't find my legs
Suppose you live and learn
Learn it again and again

Smack in the middle of today
Got to find new words
Merely got to simply say
I think we all misheard

Just like my lower heaven
You know so well my higher hell
(When confronted by continuing the course)
(Will you open up or do I have to force)
(The words right out)
(Of your stubborn mouth)
(Stunted of course)
(Guilty in their growth)

from the album 'Porcupine' 4/2/1983

HISTORY CHIMES

Bells high on a hill
History chimes
And you want a new beginning
Tell me in biro or quill
Your purpose and mine
Prove that our world is spinning
So here goes nothing better
And here's to something else

  Until tomorrow
  But that's another time
  It's just another time
  It's just some other troubled time

The seed grew up a boy
Turned to a man
Is this the world you wanted?
It seems under the soil
Over the sand
Not quite the seed I planted
I've seen you
And now I know better
I've been you
Now I'm someone else

  Until tomorrow
  But that's another time
  It's just another time
  It's just some other troubled time

Until tomorrow
Until...

from the album 'What Are You Going To Do With Your Life?' 16/4/1999

HOLY GRAIL

There's a broken-down castle
With blood on the battlements
You know how it's gonna end
With a forgotten angel
Who'll never be able
To soar with the gods again

You never know
N-n-no...

There's a plague in the wind
That's sweeping us in
With a sadness that comes to us all
At the edge of a cliff
Is a bottomless pit
Where all of us have to fall

All the kings and queens
And knights in shining armour
All the holy ghosts
And all our holy fathers

Take what's yours and take it boldly
And boldly go where you tread so coldly
The drop is sheer and never holy
Just you and you alone
Ride the wave when it comes crashing
Be the knight in a shining costume
Slay the dragons if they're asking
For what you've always known

All the kings and queens
And knights in shining armor
All the holy ghosts
And all our holy fathers

Gotta get me in...

There's a broken-down castle
With blood on the battlements
You know how it's gonna end
With a forgotten angel
Who'll never be able
To soar with the gods again
There's a plague in the wind
That's sweeping us in
With a sadness that comes to us all
At the edge of a cliff
Is a bottomless pit
Where all of us have to fall

And someone above
Is handing down love
Putting a twist in the tale
And left it too late
For someone who hates
To get to the holy grail

Come inside...

from the album 'Burned' 1/10/1995

HONEYDRIP

It's in my mind
In my body and soul
Stuck in the I can't understand
They're selling me views
Waving my flagpole
Donating my eyes
Tying my hands

  Drip honeydrip, drip your innocence
  Drip, honey, drip through the night
  Drip honeydrip, drip your inner sense
  'Cos I'm feeling guilty tonight

Madness comes and then madness goes
Another warship in the night
Know your God, hope Heaven knows
Your wrong from His right

  And drip honeydrip, drip your innocence
  Drip over me through the night
  Drip, honey, drip, drip your inner sense
  'Cos I'm feeling guilty tonight

It's Guy Fawlkes night, pistols at dawn
Let's walk upon the misty moors
If luck runs out I'll go and buy some more
Chance for the chancers
Fate for the poor

It's in my mind, in my body and soul
It's in my mind, body and soul...

You can't always get what you want
You can't always get what you want
No you can't always get what you want
But if you try sometimes
You just might find
That it's in your mind
Body and soul
It's in my mind
Body and soul...
Body and soul

from the album 'Mysterio' 17/3/1992

HORSE'S HEAD

A single rose
The curtains closed
A stranger's clothes
Were all I found
The great unknown
The tightrope show
A world below
Don't look down
Don't look down
Don't look down

Horse's head found in a bed
Broke the code and braved the weather
Wore a gown of chestnut brown
Fingers crossed that there's a Heaven

Heaven...

Found a scroll
And ancient bones
A million ghosts
Were all around
The great unknown
The tightrope show
A world below
Don't look down
Don't look down
Don't look down

Horse's head found in a bed
Broke the code and braved the weather
Wore a gown of chestnut brown
Fingers crossed that there's a Heaven

Heaven...

I found a scroll
And ancient bones
A million ghosts were all around...

from the album 'Candleland' 17/9/1989

I KNOW YOU WELL

Is your mind made up or willing
To be changed or to stay true?
Are you primed to make the killing
Or too scared to follow through?
When all the blood is spilling
Will it be to real for you?

I know you well
I know you well
I know you well
Yes I know you well

When everything is hollow
Holiness will call for you
And I will have to follow
And you will follow too
Will all those silver dollars
Be enough to see us through?

They know us well
They know us well
They know us well
Yes they know us well

Is your mind made up or willing
To be changed, stay true?
Are you primed to make the killing
Or too scared to follow through?
When all the blood is spilling
Will it pour right out of you?

You know me well
You know me well
You know me well
Yes you know me well

You know me well

from the album 'Candleland' 17/9/1989

I'LL FLY TONIGHT

I'm gonna lift you up
I'm gonna lie you down
I'm gonna be the king of kings
You're gonna rise above
All of the other stuff
You'll be the queen of everything

Nothing's gonna be the same
Nothing's gonna be the same

I'll fly tonight
I'll fly tonight
Into your light

I'm gonna mess you up
I'm gonna let you down
I'm gonna cut you to the bone
You're gonna lose your nerve
You're gonna learn to hate
You'll have a love you've never known

Nothing's ever gonna change
Nothing's ever gonna change

I'll fly tonight
I'll fly tonight
Into your light...

If I should fall from some great height
Will I be caught mid-flight?
If I should steer us far and long
Will you be near when I go wrong?

I'm gonna lift you up
I'm gonna lie you down
I'm gonna be the king of kings

Nothing's gonna be the same
Nothing's ever gonna change

from the album 'Evergreen' 14/7/1997

IN BLOOM

Think twice
And do it
Stale life
Don't chew it
Cloud lands
Fog reason
Blue skies
Wrong season

So soon
Vanishing days
Perfume
Of old bouquets

Rice fields
Feet soaking
Minefields
Here's hoping

So soon
Vanishing days
Perfume
Of old bouquets

In bloom...

Think twice
And do it
Stale life
Don't chew it
Cloud lands
Fog reason
Blue skies
Wrong season

So soon
Vanishing days
Perfume
Of dead bouquets

In bloom...

from the album 'Candleland' 17/9/1989

IN BLUER SKIES

What needs must be
I realised
I'm walking out
From blackened skies

You say belief
Is in our eyes
But how can I believe
In blind lies

  I'm counting
  On your heavy heart
  Could it keep me
  From falling apart

Have we been born to follow
Tied to a bitter rein
Or will we begin to grow
Bound by this simple chain

Will we evolve tonight
Sparkle like brittle stars
Can we dissolve tonight
Held by your hungry arms

  I'm counting
  On your heavy heart
  Could it keep me
  From falling apart

I would be ready
Ready to go
Was your heart heavy
Heavy with sorrow
Had you been ready
We could have both been grown
Now your hearts heavy
Heavy with sorrow

I'm counting
On your heavy heart
Could it keep me
From falling apart

What needs have been
You'll realize
I've found myself
In bluer skies

I know belief
Is in your eyes
We can't believe
In blind lies

I'm counting
On your heavy heart
To keep me
From falling apart

from the album 'Porcupine' 4/2/1983

IN MY HEAD

Round and round
(Deliver)
All the things in my head
(Me from good)
Round and round
(Deliver)
Did the things you said
(Me from good)

On and on and on and on
(A to Z)
On and on and on...
(Good as dead)

In my head
Things went 'round
In my head
I fell down

Come and gone
All the things we did
Nights so long
Those things well hid

On and on and on and on
On and on and on...

In my head
Things went 'round
In my head
I fell down
Down...

In my in my in my head
In my in my in my head

from the album 'Mysterio' 17/3/1992

IN MY TIME

On your wings you'll carry me down
Highways to the shore
And at your wheel you'll steer me
Then steer me no more
Me no more

All my leaves are turning
With the changing of the seasons
And all my dreams are burning up
And looking for a reason

In my time of living I just wanted to be true
But I just took your giving and I stole the truth from you
And in the line of duty
I turned upon my heels
Peeled the skin off beauty
And too much was revealed
Much too real

All my pages empty
Like a book I never read
And all my words are words I wish
Wish I could have said

All my leaves are turning
With the changing of the seasons
And all my dreams are burning up
And running out of reasons
All my pages empty like a book I never read
And all my words are words I wish
Wish I never said

Hitching a ride
Down your highway...

from the album 'Evergreen' 14/7/1997

IN THE MARGINS

Tuck me in
I need to sleep now
I need dream how
I used to dream

Look me in
Look me in the face now
Help me believe how
I used to believe

 Now do you see how
 There in the margins
 Below and up above
 I see now
 How life wins
 When all that's left is love

Rope me in
Lasso my heart, love
Noose up my soul, love
Spirits in chains

Hope begins
Right at the start of
The search for the gold, love
Died in the rain

 Now do you see how
 We're in the margins
 We're below and up above
 I see now
 How life wins
 When we're all that's left of love

We're all that's left
Of love
We're all that's left
Of love

Tuck me in
I need to sleep now
I need dream how
I used to dream

Look me in
Look me in the face now
Help me believe how
I used to believe

Now do you see how
They're in the margins
Below and up above
I see now
How life wins
When all that's left is love

All that's left is love
All that's left of love

from the album 'Siberia' 20/9/2005

IT WAS A PLEASURE

Let's get rid of the shit
I know you'd like that, too
The stuff that undermines
The best of me and you

It was a pleasure to meet you
You slapped me right on the back
Just a pleasure to meet you
You got it almost exact

No discussion now
No bad dreams now
No reason now
No excuses now

If I knock it all back
Just like you said I do
Would it confirm the suspect?
The suspicion will do

It was a pleasure to meet you
You slapped me right on the back
Just a pleasure to meet you
You got it almost exact

No discussion now
No illusion now
No dilution now
No excuses now

Let's get rid of the shit
I know you like that, too
The stuff that undermines
The best of me and you

Failure to do so will result in the failure
Failure to do so will result in the failure

from the album 'Heaven Up Here' 30/5/1981

IT'S ALRIGHT

Somebody wants you
Someone out there
Somebody needs you
Somebody cares
Somebody loves you
Someone somewhere
But if nobody's there

Here they come again
Whispers in my head
Same old sad refrain
Wish'd I'd never said
What I said... yeah
Take me to the top
I need more not less
And don't ever tell me when to stop

Here comes tomorrow
And yesterday's news
Empty and hollow
Broken and bruised
No one to follow, nothing to lose
And only you can choose

Here they come again
Whispers in my head
Same old sad refrain
Wish'd I'd never said
What I said... yeah
Take me to the top
I need more not less
And don't ever tell me when to stop

Here they come again
Whispers in my head
Same old sad refrain
Wish'd I'd never said
What I said......yeah
Take me to the top
I need more not less
And don't ever tell me when to stop

Somebody wants you
Someone out there
Somebody needs you
Somebody cares
Somebody loves you
Someone somewhere
But if nobody's there

Here they come again
Whispers in my head
Same old sad refrain
Wish'd I'd never said
What I said......yeah
Take me to the top
I need more not less
And don't ever tell me when to stop

from the album 'Flowers' 16/2/2001

I WANT TO BE THERE (WHEN YOU COME)

I wanna be like you
I wanna fly, fly, fly
Want you to take me to
All of your sky

Why don't you wear me down
Why don't you try, try, try
'Cos when you come around
That's when I fly

'Cos I don't wanna go under
It's only just begun

  I wanna be there when you come
  I wanna be there when you come

I wanna be like you
I wanna laugh and cry
About the things we do
And never ask why

'Cos I don't wanna go under
It's only just begun

  I wanna be there when you come
  I wanna be there when you come

I wanna be like you
I wanna fly, fly, fly
Want you to take me to
All of your sky
I wanna paint the town
And drink it dry, dry, dry
And when the lights go down
I'll say goodbye

To all the rain and the thunder
I'm heading into the sun

  I wanna be there when you come
  I wanna be there when you come

from the album 'Evergreen' 14/7/1997

JUST A TOUCH AWAY

You said you could make it disappear
Make my pathway clean and my pathway clear
You said I was just a touch away
But I'm not even close
No, I'm nowhere near

How d'you wanna go?
Should we go together?
I don't wanna go
I'm gonna live forever
Live forever

The shadows and the fog are moving in
From the world outside to my world within
I'm sucking on the dust that moves the air
The pieces move but I'm still there
Shadows and the fog are moving in
From the world outside to my world within

How d'you want to go
Calm or stormy weather?
If we've gotta go
Let's go together
Together...

Live forever...

from the album 'Evergreen' 14/7/1997

KANSAS

Coming up
Coming into view
Come and see what I've become
I'm saving up my souvenirs for you
You can take them when I'm gone

Where I'm heading I can't tell
Down to Heaven
Or up to Hell

And if who we are is who we love
Then who put all this hate inside me?
And if who we are is written in the stars
When's someone gonna come and find me?

I'm growing up
Growing into me
Knowing now where I come from
I'm going back, going back to see
How going right could go so wrong.

Where I'm heading I can't tell
Down to Heaven
Or up to Hell

And if who we are is who we love
Then who put all this hate inside me?
And if who we are is written in the stars
When's someone gonna come and find me?

Where the jewels will be revealed
Where the jewels the river gives in the pool where we live
In the glow of shadows magic waters flow

Burning up
Burning up inside
I don't want to feel the cold
I'm turning 'round
Turning 'round to find
All that glitter turned to gold
Where I'm heading I can't tell
Not to Heaven
And not to Hell

And if who we are is who we love
Then who put all this hate inside me?
And if who we are is written in the stars
When's someone gonna come and find me?

from the album 'Slideling' 28/4/2003

KING OF KINGS

Met Jesus up on a hill
He confessed I was dressed to kill
Saw fear eternal in his eyes
He's seen what happens when the soul dies

I'm the King of Kings
Wearing broken wings
I've lost my crown
The world so far below
And all I really know
Is that you don't look down

Came alive in the dead of night
Sought salvation in the city lights
One more drink, and one drink more
Every hour like the one before

I'm the King of Kings
Wearing broken wings
I've lost my crown
The world so far below
And all I really know
Is that you don't look down

Don't look down
It's such a long way to fall

Came alive in the dead of night
Sought salvation in the city lights
One more drink, and one drink more
Every hour like the one before

You're like me, and I'm like you
Can't see the point in a point of view
All time lows we're hitting the heights
Two wrongs tryin' to make it alright

I'm the King of Kings
Wearing broken wings
I've lost my crown
The world so far below
And all I really know
Is that you don't look down

from the album 'Flowers' 16/2/2001

LIFE OF A THOUSAND CRIMES

If I changed along the way
Is there a price that I can pay?
Just tell me all I have to say is save me

Just tell me it'll be okay
That tomorrow won't be like today
Don't make me have to kneel and pray
For maybes.... just save me

I heard it a thousand times
Life of a thousand crimes

Don't want to know what I've become
Just want the wrongs I've done undone
I need more than just the crumbs you gave me

I want a place where I can run
I want a race that can be won
I want a face and a golden sun to bathe me

I heard it a thousand times
Life of a thousand crimes

Do you want to know?
What I know?

Do you want to go?
Really want to go?
Do you want to go where I go?

from the album 'The Fountain' 12/10/2009

LIPS LIKE SUGAR

She floats like a swan
Grace on the water
Lips like sugar
Lips like sugar
Just when you think you've caught her
She glides across the water
She calls for you tonight
To share this moonlight

You'll flow down her river
She'll ask you and you'll give her

Lips like sugar
Sugar kisses
Lips like sugar
Sugar kisses

She knows what she knows
I know what she's thinking
Sugar kisses
Sugar kisses
Just when you think she's yours
She's flown to other shores
To laugh at how you break
And melt into this lake

You'll flow down her river
But you'll never give her

Lips like sugar
Sugar kisses
Lips like sugar
Sugar kisses

She'll be my mirror
Reflect what I am
A loser and winner
The King of Siam I am
And my Siamese twin
Alone on the river
Mirror kisses
Mirror kisses

Lips like sugar
Sugar kisses
Lips like sugar
Sugar kisses

Lips like sugar
Sugar kisses
Lips like sugar
Sugar kisses

Lips like sugar
Sugar kisses
Lips like sugar
Sugar kisses

from the album 'Echo & The Bunnymen' 6/7/1987

LOST AND FOUND

I was standing in a graveyard
under silver studded skies
In a forest burning ashes
on the bonfires of our lives

As the sky fell down
I was lost and found
saw my world spin round
round and round

All the ghosts have gathered round me
come to tell me of a change
in the darkness that surrounds me
I am falling down again

On this haunted ground
I was lost and found

Lost, lost and found
Lost, lost and found

She will tell you her cathedral
has no windows and no doors
and you know she doesn't need you
and that's why you want her more

As your heart melts down
you are lost not found

Lost, lost and found
Lost, lost and found

I was counting all the tombstones
of the buried boys and girls
as the wind blew in like ice
and froze this cemetery world

And we all fell down
we were lost and found

Lost, lost and found
Lost, lost and found

from the album 'Echo & The Bunnymen' 6/7/1987

LOST ON YOU

It's just a dangerous bend
On a slippery slope
Another rainbow's end
On the highway of hope
It's always next time
Always next time
Always last time

Just get me out of this jam
It's stuck to me like glue
And I can't remember who I am
My memory got lost on you

I had things inside my head
And they put me behind them
Thought they'd be safe in my head
And now I just can't find them

It's just a trick of light
And some sleight of hand
Another kiss goodnight
Along the rise of man
And it's the last time
It's the last time
'Til the next time

So get me out of this jam
It's stuck to me like glue
And I can't remember who I am
My memory got lost on you

I had things inside my head
And they put me behind them
Thought they'd be safe in my head
And now I just can't find them

It's gone and that's too bad
The best thing that I ever had
Had the whole world in my mouth
Ate it up and spat it out...

from the album 'What Are You Going To Do With Your Life?' 16/4/1999

LOVE IN VEINS

Really really want you
Yeah I really really need you
And I've really really got you under my skin
In my skin in my skin in my skin

Early in the morning
And nearly every evening
I get those early early warnings
Coming in, coming in, coming in

Can you feel it? Is it living?
Can you touch it? Is it loving?
Is it loving?
Got you in my sun-sun

Yeah I got you in my rain
And I got you in my blood-blood
Love in veins, love in veins, love in veins

Can you feel it? Is it living?
Can you touch it? Is it loving?
Is it loving?

from the album 'Slideling' 28/4/2003

LOWDOWN

It's the twists and the turns of the cigarette burns
The holes in the mind of the nebulous mass
You'll get no returns if you don't learn
The diff between mine and the hole in your past
Every city we've been in
Built on the dust of someone's ash
When I die I'm gonna die 'cos of living
See you in hell with the rest of the trash

I need a love a love without question
A clean mind and a pocket of space
I want a map and a sense of direction
Looking for love and the thrill of a world

Just spinning 'round
Trynna burn
But you're melting down
You wanna be up there
But you're underground
Do you feel it lowdown?

Too many thoughts put a twist in my thinking
I just can't think straight anymore
I've got the bends I can feel myself sinking
Just can't keep on keep on coming back for more
Hey love, there's no need to worry
I've got nails, so hold on hold on
Think back before you started thinking about
The things you were sold on sold on

Can you spin it 'round?
Trynna hold on
But you nail it down
You wanna be up there
But you're underground

Do you feel it lowdown?
Lowdown...

And the world keeps spinning 'round
Trynna burn
But you melt it down
You wanna be out there
But you're underground

Do you feel it lowdown?

Spinning 'round...
Ghost riders in the sky
Lowdown...

from the album 'Burned' 1/10/1995

MAKE ME SHINE

I'll be with you, in your summer
Winter spring and fall days
You and me, yeah we've got each other
I'll be there... always

  Love it when you say
  I'm the gold inside your goldmine
  And I love the way
  You just make me shine

When our ship hits stormy weather
We'll ride the tidal waves
You and me sailing seas together
In the same boat... always

  Love it when you say
  I'm the gold inside your goldmine
  And I love the way
  You just make me shine

I'll be with you, in your summer
Winter spring and fall days
You and me, yeah we've got each other
I'll be there... always

  Love it when you say
  I'm the gold inside your goldmine
  And I love the way
  You just make me shine

from the album 'Flowers' 16/2/2001

MAKE US BLIND

Something got me thinking tonight about
Changes
Changes

Somebody bought me a ticket tonight
Dangerous
Dangers

I've just gotta go...

Where everything is what it could be now
Where everything is ready for me now
Everything and every time
Everything and every kind
Make me yours
I'll make you mine
Make us blind

Someone asked me something tonight,
What my name is, game is

Somebody made me feel something tonight
Blameless, painless

I've just gotta know...

from the album 'Siberia' 20/9/2005

MAGICAL WORLD

Raining down on me and it's no wonder why
I feel so low
'Cos it's down to you
You sucked away the faith I used to have in me
And it's fallen through
Yeah it's fallen through
You pump me full of holes
You pump me full of holes

  And all I want to know is
  Is it really such a magical world?
  Is it really such a magical world?
  Magical world...

Swept out in the wind it's me as castaway
There's no ship to sail
Washed me up on shore
You pointed to my star and then it blew away
And you said to me
That's what stars are for
They fill you full of holes
Silver shining holes

  And all I want to know is
  Is it really such a magical world?
  Is it really such a magical world?...
  Magical world...

from the album 'Mysterio' 17/3/1992

MARBLE TOWERS

Spent the night in marble towers
A million stories high
Saw the lights of meteor showers
Dropping in the sky
Made a wish and wished I'd made it
Home before the sun
Running for the rooftops
Rooftop's on the run

Don't think twice and roll the dice
Stake your life on a perfect seven
Paradise at any price
Take your slice for a piece of Heaven

Left the life the life you left me
Crying out for more
Guess you knew you knew I guessed it
What those clues were for
Maps for dreams, hiding places
Underneath the stairs
Hiding in the rooftops
Rooftop's running scared

Don't look twice and roll the dice
Stake your life on a perfect seven
Paradise at any price
Take another slice get a piece of Heaven
Heaven...

b side from the single 'It's Alright' 23/4/2001

MIRRORBALL

All the world is sleeping
I can't close my eyes
Watch the darkness deepen
One more time to die
I wanna be redeemed
I need a new surpriseFeeling good-for-nothing
Tastes like salt and rain
Feel the same as you
Say you feel the sameI got it, I got it good
On my white-knuckle ride
Oh yeah, if only I could
Get out the other side
Feels like a nightmare in my head
Feels like there's something going down
Feels like an earthquake in my mind
Feels like an earthquake...Helter skelter shelter
The freak show's inside
I'm a mirrorball
You're the guiding lightI got it, I got it good
On my white-knuckle ride
If only, if I could
Find somewhere else to hide

from the album 'Burned' 1/10/1995

MONKEYS

I bagsy yours
If you'll bagsy mine
I'll take a chance
If you'll take the blame
Forget it
Forget it

Keymon
Keymon

Boys are the same
Brains in their pockets
Girls are the same
Knock it and rock it
Remember
Remember

Keymon
Keymon

I'm not a holy man
I'm too lowly for that
I'm not a praying man
I'm not ready for that

Keymon
Keymon

I bagsy yours
If you'll bagsy mine
I'll take a chance
If you'll take the blame
Forget it
Forget it

Keymon
Keymon Keymon
Keymon

from the album 'Crocodiles' 18/7/1980

MORNING SUN

Show me the hole I can fall in
To the ground to the ground to the ground
Speak to me speak and give me my calling
'Cos I'm going down, going down, going down

  It's only lies and alibis
  Alibis and lies
  We know something dies every day

I've lost or I've forgotten
More than I'll ever know
Born just a someone with some kind of nothing
I let it go, let it go, let it go

  It's only lies and alibis
  Alibis and lies
  We know something dies every day
  Here it comes the morning sun
  Another hit and run
  And we're just the ones in the way

Coming down with you...

Give me a hope I can lean on
'Cos I'll bend in the calmest of winds
Give me more than dreams for me to dream on
My jury's in, coming in, coming in...

from the album 'What Are You Going To Do With Your Life?' 16/4/1999

MY KINGDON

I chop and I change and the mystery thickens
There's blood on my hands and you want me to listen
To brawn and to brain when the truth's in the middle
Born of the grain like all good riddles

  B-b-burn the skin off and climb the roof top
  Thy will be done
  B-b-bite the nose off and make it the most of
  Your king- kingdom kingdom kingdom

You kill when you talk and the enemy weakens
Your words start to walk when you're not even speaking
If my heart is a war its soldiers are bleeding
If my heart is a war its soldiers are dead

  B-b-b-burn the skin off and climb the roof top
  Thy will be done
  B-b-bite the nose off and make it the most of
  Your king- kingdom kingdom kingdom

I've lost and I've gained and while I was thinking
You cut off my hands when I wanted to twist
If you know how to dance tell Boney Maroney
He's doing the ballet on both of his wrists

  B-b-b-burn the skin off and climb the roof top
  Thy will be done
  B-b-bite the nose off and make it the most of
  Your k- k- k- k- k- kingdom, king- k- k- k- k-

  B-b-b-burn the skin off and climb the roof top
  And I will be done
  B-b-bite the nose off and make the most of
  Your king- kingdom, kingdom, kingdom

(You're a between the lines person)
(And your death is well overdue)
(You suck the foot that kicks you)
(You kiss the hand that hits you)

(You're a between the lines person)
(And your death is well overdue)
(Keep on sucking)

from the album 'Ocean Rain' 8/5/1984

MY WHITE DEVIL

John Webster was
One of the best there was
He was the author of
Two major tragedies
The White Devil and
The Duchess of Malfi
The White Devil and
The Duchess of Malfi

Change in the wether
Do I get the choice?
Chance in forever
When do we get the spoils?

Now that love is upside-down
It's down to us to say that
Our monkey brains
Content to laugh
When laughing wanes
It's time to change

Make on the when
I will be then
You on the then
We will be then

Here it comes again
Knocking on its feet
Here it comes again
Knocking on its feet

Don't say it's like I'm inferior
Don't say it's like I'm inferior
Don't say it's like I'm inferior

Is it enough now
To tell me you matter
When you haven't a clue how
To bring me to tears
How many leaves must you crumble
Till you believe what I told you
That your legs have to stubble

Change in the wether
Do I get the choice
Chance it forever
When do we get the spoils

from the album 'Porcupine' 4/2/1983

NEVER STOP

Good God, you said, is that the only thing you care about
Splitting up the money and share it out
The cake's being eaten straight through the mouth
Poison poised to come back in season
For all the ones who lack reason

 Measure by measure, drop by drop
 And pound for pound, we're taking stock
 Of all the treasures still unlocked
 The love you found must never stop

The king is dead and long live the people who aim above
All the simple stuff never understood
Like right from bad and wrong from good
Deny that you were ever tempted by the lie
That there's an answer in the sky

 Measure by measure, drop by drop
 And pound for pound, we're taking stock
 Of all the treasures still unlocked
 The love you found must never stop...

Never stop...

from the album 'Songs To Learn And Sing' 15/11/1985

NEW DIRECTION

Out on a limb
Did you see what the cat dragged in
Take it on the chin
Catching fire on a roof of tin

You've learnt to speak and you're professing
The right to teach us our direction
But I found out on close inspection
True imperfection

I'm looking for a new direction
Where in the world am I?
I took the word the word was resurrection
and then you took me out to climb

Higher and higher
Higher and higher
Higher and higher
Kissing the spires
Higher and higher
Higher and higher
Higher and higher
Souls on fire

Inside of my head
I heard what the good Lord said
"Beware" he said
If you don't you might end up dead

You suck the air right out of me
But though you suck you cannot see
That life and living are not free
Though you live you do not breathe

I'm looking for a new direction
where in the world am I?
I took the word the word was resurrection
and then you took me out to climb

  Higher and higher
  Higher and higher
  Higher and higher
  Kissing the spires
  Higher and higher
  Higher and higher
  Higher and higher
  Souls on fire

I have changed
but still my heart
remains intact
and true love stays
but will our hearts
retain their lack of

No sense and no direction
Who in the world am I?
I took the word the word was resurrection
and then you took me out to climb

  Higher and higher
  Higher and higher
  Higher and higher
  Kissing the spires
  Higher and higher
  Higher and higher
  Higher and higher
  Souls on fire

Start confessing
Start confessing

All my evils would be blessed
if to God I did confess
Wipe the slate and see if I
ate the bread and drank the wine
So as you're leaving on the great procession
just take the bottle and start confessing

from the album 'Echo & The Bunnymen' 6/7/1987

NO DARK THINGS

I like it
My hands clean
No head shaved
It's quite safe
Compromise discovery
It's just an, it's only

My good fell
Oh you miss
Construe all
The tactics

You must learn
To distin
Guish error
From your fate
They really don't think it's funny
That he's beginning to accept the facts

To the middle of the floor
You walked over
In the middle of the wall
The picture still hanging
From the corner of my eye
You stick the pins in
In the middle of the floor
I fell over

We have no dark things
Nothing to hide or that
Just some heads and a wish
Something to sing about
We have no dark things
Nothing to hide or that
Just some heads and a wish
Something to shout about
We have no dark things
Nothing to hide or that
Just some heads and a wish
Something to sing about

No dark things
No dark things
No dark things
No dark things
No dark things
No dark things
No dark things
No dark things

from the album 'Heaven Up Here' 30/5/1981

NOCTURNAL ME

An ice-cap fire
All burning wood
In a world of wire
Ignite our dreams of
Starry skies and you and me
Us realised... our bigger themes

Oh, take me internally
Forever yours
Nocturnal me
Take me internally
Forever yours
Nocturnal me

Do or die
What's done is done
True beauty lies
On the blue horizon

Who or why
What's won is won
In pure disguise
Of vulgar sons

Oh, take me internally
Forever yours
Nocturnal me
Take me internally
Forever yours
Nocturnal me

Whatever burns burns eternally
So take me in turns internally
When I'm on fire
My body will be
Forever yours
Nocturnal me

An ice-capped fire
All burning wood
In a world of wire
Ignite our dreams of starry skies
And you and me
Us realised our bigger themes

Oh, take me internally
Forever yours
Nocturnal me
Take me internally
Forever yours
Nocturnal me

from the album 'Ocean Rain' 8/5/1984

NOTHING LASTS FOREVER

I want it now, I want it now
Not the promises of what tomorrow brings
I need to live in dreams today
I'm tired of the song that sorrow sings

And I want more than I can get
Just trying to, trying to, trying to
Forget

I'd walk to you through rings of fire
But never let you know the way I feel
Under skin is where I hide
The love that always gets me on my knees

And I want more than I can get
Just trying to, trying to, trying to
Forget

 Nothing ever lasts forever...

I want it now, I want it now
Don't tell me that my ship is coming in
Nothing comes to those who wait
Time's running out the door you're running in

And I want more than I can get
Just trying to, trying to, trying to
Forget

 Nothing ever lasts forever...

All the shadows and the pain
Are coming to you...

Yeah yeah yeah...

from the album 'Evergreen' 14/7/1997

NOT OF THIS WORLD

God, look at you
Shining through
You could be somebody
Good, almost new
Someone who
Could be anybody

Not of this world
Of this town
Of this house you call home
Born out of time
Out of place
Out there on your own

In the beginning
And then out at the death
I'll be walking behind you
And be next breath

b side from the single 'Never' 22/10/1995

OCEAN RAIN

All at sea again
And now my hurricane's brought down this ocean rain
To bathe me again
My ship's asail can you hear it's tender frame
Screaming from beneath the waves
Screaming from beneath the waves

  All hands on deck at dawn
  Sailing to sadder shores
  Your port in my heavy storm
  Harbours the blackest thoughts

I'm at sea again
And now your hurricanes
Will bring down my Ocean Rain
To bathe us again
My ship's asail can you hear it's tender frame
Screaming from beneath your waves
Screaming from beneath your waves

  All hands on deck at dawn
  Sailing to sadder shores
  Your port in my heavy Storm
  Harbours the blackest thoughts

All at sea again
And now our hurricanes
Have brought down this Ocean Rain
To bathe us again.

My ship's a sail can you hear it's tender frame
Screaming from beneath the waves
Screaming from beneath your waves
Screaming from beneath the waves

from the album 'Ocean Rain' 8/5/1984

OF A LIFE

Is this how the end begins?
Infra-reds and ultra-violets
No one there to mend your wings
Flown by unconscious pilot

Tell me I'm not seein' things
Say it's love I've sighted
I wanna song to learn and sing
Of a love requited

This is where the beggin' ends
No more Trevi fountains
No more kneelin', no more bends
No more jumpin' off the mountain

Tell me I'm not seein' things
Say it's love I've sighted
I wanna song to learn and sing
Of a life requited

Of a life requited
Of a life requited
Of a life requited

No more time and childish things
No more time for wasting
Now its time to find the things
I'm forever chasin'

Tell me I'm not seein' things
Say it's love I've sighted
I wanna song to learn and sing
Of a life requited

Tell me I'm not seein' things
Say it's love I've sighted
wanna song to learn and sing
of a love requited

Of a life requited
Of a life requited
Of a love requited
Of a life requited
Of a life requited

from the album 'Siberia' 20/9/2005

OVER THE WALL

The man at the back has a question
His tongue's involved with solutions
But the monkey on my back
Won't stop laughing

  Over the wall
  Hand in hand
  Over the wall
  Watch us fall

There's something to be said for you
And your hopes of higher ruling
But the slug on my neck
Won't stop chewing

  Over the wall
  Hand in hand
  Over the wall
  Watch us fall

I'm walking in the rain
To end this misery
I'm walking in the rain
To celebrate this misery
What's that you say?
Speak up, I can't hear you
What did you say?
I couldn't hear you

  Over the wall
  Hand in hand
  Over the wall
  Watch us fall

Pounding the road coast to coast
Pounding the road coast to coast

I'm over the wall
I'm over the wall
I'm over the wall
Come over the wall
Come over the wall

I can't sleep at night
How I wish you'd hold me tight
I can't sleep at night
Come on and hold me tight...

I can't sleep at night
How I wish you'd hold me tight
Come on and hold me tight

I can't sleep at night
How I wish you'd hold me tight
Come on and hold me tight
Come on and hold me tight

I can't sleep at night
How I wish you'd hold me tight
Hold me tight
Hold me tight
IIold mc tight
To my logical limit
To the logical limit
To my logical limit
To the logical limit

from the album 'Heaven Up Here' 30/5/1981

OVER YOU

Jump right in
take the call
were you pushed
or did you fall?
Fell apart
Feeling low
happy ride
the merry-go

 And I always hear them singing
 and complaining about the world
 but my chiming bells are ringing out
 the word the word the word

Love rebounds
heart goes snap
Is she ever
coming back?
Let her down
break her fall
never ever
Felt so small

 And I always hear them singing
 and complaining about the world
 and my chiming bells are ringing out
 the word the word the word

Feeling good again
always hoped I would
never believed
that I ever could
Feeling blue again
never wanted to
Under the weather
And it's over you

Over you (the hole in the holy)
(and the crack in our hearts)
Over you (it's love and love only)
(that sets our world apart)
Over you (worlds apart)
(joined at the heart)

Jump right in
take the call
Were you pushed
Or did you fall?
Fell apart
Feeling low
Happy ride
the merry-go

And I always hear them singing
and complaining about the world
and my chiming bells are ringing out
the word the word the word

Feeling good again
always hoped I would
never believed
that I ever could
Felling blue again
never wanted to
Under the weather
And it's over you

Over you (the hole in the holy)
(and the crack in our hearts)
Over you (it's love and love only)
(the sets our worlds apart)

Feeling good again
always hoped I would
never believed
that I ever could
Felling blue again
never wanted to
Under the weather
And it's over you

Over you (and a dream is a means)
(to an end of the things)
Over you (that will tempt you away)
(From the path to the true way in)

Feeling good again
always hoped I would
never believed
that I ever could
Felling blue again
never wanted to
Under the weather
And it's over you

Over you
Over you

from the album 'Echo & The Bunnymen' 6/7/1987

OVER YOUR SHOULDER

Look over your shoulder
I'm here
The face on your head looks older
We're here

  Never gonna change
  Never gonna disappear
  Stars shine down on me tonight
  Doors close tight

The day of departure
Is near
The ears on your head
Don't hear

  Never gonna change
  Never gonna disappear
  Stars shine down on me tonight
  Doors close tight

Victims fall
Ghosts descend
You get scared and I'll pretend
I really care then I'll defend
The good and bad right to the end

Look in the cellar
We're here
I've been meaning to tell you
I'm here

  Never gonna change
  Never gonna disappear
  Stars shine down on me tonight
  Doors close tight

Victims fall
Ghosts descend
You get scared and I'll pretend
I don't really care but I'll defend
The good and band right to the end
End...

Look over your shoulder
I'm here
The face on your head looks over
We're here

Never gonna change
Never gonna disappear
Stars shine down on me tonight
Doors close tight

b side from the single 'Bring On The Dancing Horses' 14/11/1985

PARTHENON DRIVE

There I am
Must have been just five
Five parts alive
On Parthenon Drive

Pencils and pen-knives
On Parthenon Drive

Years turned
Into an eight
And you made me wait
At the garden gate
And you were always late
When I was eight

Clocks hit twelve
And dreams will fall
Off my shelves
And off my walls

Turned into
A twenty two
And airplanes flew
When I was twenty two
And growing pains grew
When I was twenty two

Spinning round a thirty three
Trying to find
The worth in me
Yeah trying to find
Gave all the earth to be

Clocks hit twelve
And dreams will fall
Off my shelves
And off my walls

Revolving round
A forty five
Glad to be alive
Around a forty five
Yeh glad to be alive
Around a forty five

Here I am
The age of five
Five parts alive
On Parthenon Drive
Glad to be alive
From Parthenon Drive

from the album 'Siberia' 20/9/2005

PICTURES ON MY WALL

Can you hear it?
The sound of something burning
Something changing
On the merry-go-round tonight

The pictures on my wall
Are about to swing and fall
Love it all, love it all

Ooh, we should have
Should have got it right
Ooh, we should have
Should have got it right tonight

People come
I count every one
Faces burning, hearts beating
Nowhere left for us to run

The pictures on my wall
Are about to swing and fall
Love it all, love it all

Ooh, we should have
Should have got it right
Ooh, we should have
Should have got it right tonight

Can you hear it
The sound of someone thinking
Someone changing
On the merry-go-round tonight

The pictures on my wall
Are about to swing and fall
Love it all, love it all

from the album 'Crocodiles' 18/7/1980

PLAYGROUNDS AND CITYPARKS

In playgrounds and city parks
We played around 'til it went dark
In every breath another spark was dying
At bus stops we stood in lines
Like full stops at the end of time
Where teardrops don't ever dry for crying

Light up my life
All my days, all my nights
Light up my lonely life
Light up my lonely life

I knew I'd never leave the street
I love the taste of self-defeat
You never win and you can't beat what's broken
If you don't play then you can't lose
You either pray or have to choose
The words to say or leave the words unspoken

Light up my life
All my days, all my nights
Light up my lonely life
Light up my lonely life

In sight again and suffering
All your dreams have ended

Light up my life
All my days, all my nights
Light up my lonely life
Light up my lonely life
Light up my lonely life

from the album 'Siberia' 20/9/2005

POMEGRANATE

On one
Stretching dimensions
My brain so full of tension
And things I cannot mention
That got me on my knees

Far forgone
Along with my conclusions
That came with much confusion
And led to my delusion
But got me on my way
Got me on my way...

  Yes
  And the world fell down
  When the moon was blue
  And you wore a crown
  And the word was true

Stop it
Don't live in the gutter
Spread your bread with butter
Enunciate don't stutter
And think before you say

Drop it
String it up and eat it
Be so glad to meet it
Turn around and greet it
Make sure you get your way...

  Yes
  And the world fell down
  When the moon was blue
  And you wore a crown
  And the word was true
  True...

from the album 'Mysterio' 17/3/1992

PORCUPINE

There is no comparison
Between things about to happen
Missing the point of our mission
Will we become misshapen?

A change of heart
Will force the veil
Nailed to the door
To all avail

There are no divisions
Between things about to collide
Hitting the floor with our vision
A focus at some point arrives

A change of mind
Will force the nail
To hit the head
And set the sails

A change of skin
Will shed the tail
Hung on the wall
For use again

A change of heart
Will force the nail...
There is no comparison
Between things about to happen

Sick as a pig this pork is mine
I'm pining for the pork of the porcupine
I'd best be on my best behavior
Best behave yourself, you hear?...

Sick as a pig this pork is mine
Pine for the pork of the porcupine...
I'm beginning to see the light
Beginning to see the light

from the album 'Porcupine' 4/2/1983

POTS OF GOLD

I'm gonna roll down the mountain
I tried so hard to climb
And choose a different ambition
This time

One by one goes everyone
In search of little pots of gold
When each little pot is gone
They look for something else to hold
Heads in the sand
Sinking sand

I'm gonna jump in that fountain
And drink it 'til it's dry
'Til all that I've been missing
Is mine

One by one goes everyone
Believing all, we're taught and told
The human race in the marketplace
I'll be bought and you'll be sold
Heads in the sand
Sinking sand

Don't tell me that you're happy
No-one's happy with themselves
We all want to be somebody
Somebody else

Pots of gold...

b side from the single 'Proud To Fall' 21/8/1989

PRIDE

Mother says
Sister says
D'you mind if we laugh at you
D'you mind if we sing with you

Daddy says
Brother says
Make us proud of you
Do something we can't do

Do it, do it
Do it, do it
Do it

John waits
Barry hates
They think I'm heading for a fall
They hope I'm heading for a fall

Peter says
Julie says
I think it's time you stopped stalling
We think it's time you started falling
Fall

Mother says
Sister says
D'you mind if we laugh at you
D'you mind if we sing with you

Daddy says
Brother says
Make us proud of you
Do something we can't do

Do it, do it, do it, do it
Do it, do it, do it, do it
Do it, do it

from the album 'Crocodiles' 18/7/1980

PRO PATRIA MORI

A friend of mine
In the firing line
Got shooting pains
Ten plus nine
Not enough time
For growing pains

He had bills to pay
And foes to slay
I asked him why he bled
And this is what he said

How sweet it is
(Pro Patria Mori)

Tragic you and me
By the magic tree
With our fingers crossed
A six and three
Then home for tea
We ate Albatross

We had shame to hide
Our hands were tied
Why no tears were shed?
This is what Mum said

How sweet it is
(Pro Patria Mori)

Dulce Et Decorum...

I miss those words
I never heard
You never said
The Love Unsacred
The Kiss Unsacred
The books unread

We had nights to fall
That dreams might call
If only dreams could dare
To meet me on the stairs

How sweet it is
Yeah, how sweet it is
(Pro Patria Mori)
Dulce Et Decorum Est...

from the album 'Pro Patria Mori' 3/2012

PROUD TO FALL

Here you come again
Acting like a saviour
There you go again
Talking like a stranger
You said we all must learn to face
What we're becoming
And then I saw you in the distance
Off and running

 But from start to finish
 I was proud to fall
 And I fell so deep within it
 I got lost inside it all
 Inside it all
 Inside it all

Looks like rain again
Feels like it's rained forever
Can't remember when
Don't remember whether
I ever really told you who I was
It must have been because because
Because

 From start to finish
 I was proud to fall
 And I fell so deep within it
 I got lost inside it all
 Inside it all
 Inside it all

I fell between the bruises
And the red curtain call
I prayed you'd light the fuses
And we'd burn and torch it all

Long day's journey into
Long night's journey out
Knee-deep, so deep within you
I kept and keep without

You said we all must learn to face
What we're becoming
And then I saw you in the mirror
Off and running

But from start to finish...

from the album 'Candleland' 17/9/1989

PROXY

Show me something that I've not seen before
Show me somewhere that I've not been before
You give me so much I don't want anymore
And until I get my fill
Awake on the sea, asleep on the shore
You're making me just want to keep wanting more
I'm understanding, and I'm standing under awe

Just like many, but nobody
Not like any, everybody

  Everybody, look at us now
  Everybody, look at us now
  Everybody, look at us now
  Look at us now

I love it when you say you're better than me
Like you know you're not as clever as me
You can't connect intellectually
And until I get my fill
My head is heading for the head surgery
Everything you said, you heard it from me
Your repetition's just repeating on me

Just like many, but nobody
Not like any, everybody

  Everybody, look at us now
  Everybody, look at us now
  Everybody, look at us now
  Look at us now

Am I the wrong one ?

  Everybody, look at us now
  Everybody, look at us now
  Everybody, look at us now

from the album 'The Fountain' 12/10/2009

RAINDROPS ON THE SUN

They're building telescopes to find
The proof all hope is in the mind
And gas not God is what's behind
The beginning and the ending of time
Was never sacred, never divine
Just one giant step back for mankind

Refracted light and mirror will
With chemistry and physics kill
All afterlife and miracles
Water wasn't holy or wine
And blind faith's just for the blind
And God leaves no traces behind

It's there, out of reach
In a dream not quite broken
Like a snowflake on a beach
It awaits a breaking ocean

The will to kill's the thrill it seems
As killer-teens fill T.V. screens
They're bringing back the guillotine
Don't it make you want to go blind?
Don't it make you want to go blind?
Don't it make you want to go...

Like a race on the run
Forever out of motion
Like a raindrop on the sun
To never find the ocean

It's there, out of reach
In a dream not quite broken
Like a snowflake on a beach
It awaits a breaking ocean

from the album 'Pro Patria Mori' 3/2012

RESCUE

If I said I'd lost my way
Would you sympathise
Could you sympathise?
I'm jumbled up
Maybe I'm losing my touch
I'm jumbled up
Maybe I'm losing my touch
But you know I didn't have it anyway

  Won't you come on down to my
  Won't you come on down to my rescue

Things are wrong
Things are going wrong
Can you tell that in a song
I don't know what I want anymore
First I want a kiss and then I want it all

  Won't you come on down to my
  Won't you come on down to my rescue
  Rescue, rescue, rescue

Things are wrong
Things are going wrong
Can you tell that in a song
Losing sense of those harder things
Is this the blues I'm singing?
Is this the blues I'm singing?
Is this the blues I'm singing?
Is this the blues I'm singing?

  Won't you come on down to my
  Won't you come on down to my rescue
  Is this the blues I'm singing
  Won't you come on down to my rescue

from the album 'Crocodiles' 18/7/1980

RIPENESS

I found a thing in a bedroom
Changed the shape of the world
For long enough
Got the boat 'til as far as I could
Afford it to take me
It was far enough

Mature you said at the wrong time
Wrote my age in skin 'cause age was mine
Had a field day
Smelt like roses
Harvesting my thoughts 'cos it was time

When you grasped the question
Did you miss the meaning
When you met your challenge
Did you go out fighting
We will discover
Ripeness twice over

Sing your song
Worth its weight
In god gold
Curse its fate

When you grasped the question
Did you miss the meaning
When you met your challenge
Did you go out fighting
How will we recover
Ripeness when it's over

I lost something in a big room
Changed the shape of the world
For long enough

When you grasped the question
Did you miss the meaning
When you met your challenge
Did you go out fighting
When you climbed on top
Did you fall on shadows
And then clambering off
Did you fall on rainbows

How will we recover
Ripeness when it's over
How will we recover
Ripeness when it's over

from the album 'Porcupine' 4/2/1983

RUST

Wish that you were here
Down amongst the dust
I need someone to help me
Yeah I need someone to trust
There's something in these tears
Turning me to rust
I need someone to help me
Yeah I need someone to touch

Give me one more try
And I'll come flaking back to you
I wish that you were here
I wish that it was true

I can feel the stars shooting through my heart like rain
Leaving all the scars where the pleasure turns to pain
Point me in the light of a bright and shining right direction
And then take me home again

Just when you think it's over
Just when you think it's done
Out of every nowhere
You never see it come
I know the lines are showing
I can't keep them in
Like everybody's story
It's written on the skin

Give me one last try
And I'll make it up to you
Wish that you were here
Wish that I was true

I can feel the stars shooting through my heart like rain
Leaving all the scars where the pleasure turns to pain
Point me in the light of a bright and shining right direction
And then take me home again

Everything's gonna be alright
Everything's gonna be alright, now...

Wish that you were here...

from the album 'What Are You Going To Do With Your Life' 16/4/1999

SCISSORS IN THE SAND

Ethereally mine
Magic trees
They really used to shine
My silver leaves

Bet you're wondering how
Bet you're wondering how
Bet you're wondering how
Bet you're wondering how

Scissors in the sand
Rubberised
Watch his other hand
Ventriloquised

Bet you're wondering who
Bet you're wondering who
Bet you're wondering who
Bet you're wondering who

Something on the roof
and in the Wall
My silverfishing youth
Swim don't crawl

Bet you're wondering how
Bet you're wondering how
Bet you're wondering how
Bet you're wondering how

Scissors in the sand
Rubberised
Watch his other hand
Ventriloquised

Bet you're wondering why
Bet you're wondering why
Bet you're wondering why
Bet you're wondering why

from the album 'Siberia' 20/9/2005

SCRATCH THE PAST

If you want somebody you can understand
You know that I could be your man
But if it's anybody who can hold your hand
When any old nobody can
Rising from the ashes with my head in flames
It's good to feel the fire again
Striking all the matches in our special game
Burning through old skin to play

Just don't try to catch me 'cos I'm moving too fast
Only trynna scratch the past
C'mon...

Looking for the pieces to my jigsaw man
Trynna keep the demons in
Looking for a planet I can understand
Just trynna get my world to spin

Just don't try to catch me 'cos I'm moving too fast
Only trynna scratch the past
C'mon...

b side from the single 'It's Alright' 23/4/2001

SENSE OF LIFE

Tried to see the future
Had to lose some memory
Tried to do my duty
Had to lose some dignity

Trying to make some sense of life
Trying to get straight tonight
Tonight

Let's walk into the light
The past out of mind and out of sight
Let's make our every wrong
Turn out all right

Looking for tomorrow
Trying hard to not belong
Don't know how to follow
Don't know how to go along

Trying to make some sense of life
Trying to go straight tonight
Tonight

Let's walk into the light
The past out of mind and out of sight
Let's make our every wrong
Turn out all right

Tried to see the future
Had to lose some memory
Tried to find the beauty
Had to lose some dignity

Trying to make some sense of life
Trying to go straight tonight
Tonight

Let's walk into the light
The past out of mind and out of sight
Let's make our every wrong
Turn out all right

b side from the single 'Rust' 25/3/1999

SEVEN SEAS

Stab a sorry heart
With your favourite finger
Paint the whole world blue
And stop your tears from stinging
Hear the cavemen singing
Good news they're bringing

Seven seas
Swimming them so well
Glad to see
My face among them
Kissing the tortoise shell

A longing for
Some fresher feeling
Belonging
Or just forever kneeling
Where is the sense in stealing
Without the grace to be it

Seven seas
Swimming them so well
Glad to see
My face among them
Kissing the tortoise shell

Burning my bridges
And smashing my mirrors
Turning to see if you're cowardly
Burning the witches with mother religious
You'll strike the matches and shower me
In water games
Washing the rocks below
Taught and tamed
In time with tear flow

Seven seas
Swimming them so well
Glad to see
My face among them
Kissing the tortoise shell

Seven seas
Swimming them so well
Glad to see
My face among them
Kissing the tortoise

Seven seas
Swimming them so well
Glad to see
My face among them
Kissing the tortoise shell

from the album 'Ocean Rain' 8/5/1984

SHE SINGS (ALL MY LIFE)

It's over' she's certain
The lies that they told her just made her feel older
She's running' her time is coming
It's over' she's certain
A bargain's been struck now
She knows that her luck is changing

  She sings
  All my life
  Must I wait, all my life?
  Why does it take, all my life?
  When is it coming?
  When is it coming?

She's lying in darkness and silence
The radio's playing
She lies there praying to no one
Saying to no one

  She sings
  All my life
  Must I wait, all my life?
  Why does it take, all my life?
  When is it coming?
  When is it coming?

She sings
Do do do do doot do doot do do
It's over, she's certain
The lies that they told her just made her feel colder
She's running, her time is coming

  She sings
  All my life
  Must I wait, all my life?
  Why does it take all my life?
  When is it coming?
  When is it coming?
  When is it coming?

from the album 'Slideling' 28/4/2003

SHIP OF FOOLS

In the bedroom you will find her
All your life is there
Everything you do reminds her
Step lightly and beware

Hark the herald angels singing
All the holy bells are ringing
Hark the herald angels singing
Singing singing singing

Every journey, every station
Every twist and every turn
Signposts your destination
Rivers of no return

Hark the herald angels singing
All the holy bells are ringing
Hark the herald angels singing
Singing singing singing

All aboard
Ship of fools...

Head in the stars you're heading for home
In search of dreams that you can call your own
Call your own

In the bedroom you will find her
All your life returned
She sucked you in and lit the fire
Struck you up and watched you burn

Hark the herald angels singing
All the holy bells are ringing
Hark the herald angels singing
Singing singing singing

All aboard
Ship of fools...

Head in the stars
Heading for home

b side from the single 'The Game' 1/6/1987

SHOW OF STRENGTH

Realistically
It's hard to dig it all too happily
But I can see
It's not always that real to me
A funny thing
Is always a funny thing
And though sadly things
Just get in the way

Open to suggestion
Falling over questions

Hopefully
But that's as well as maybe
A shaking hand
Won't transmit all fidelity
Your golden smile
Would shame a politician
Typically
I'll apologise next time

Bonds will break and fade
A snapping all in two
The lies that bind and tie
Come sailing out of you

Realistically,
Hard to dig it all too happily
But I can see,
Not always that real to me
A funny thing

Is always a funny thing
And those sadly things
Is always a sadly thing

Bonds will break and fade
A snapping all in two
The lies that bind and tie
Come sailing out of you

A show of strength
Is all you want
You can never set it down...

Guts and passion
Those things you can't
Even set down
All those things you think might count
You can't ever set them down
Don't ever set them down
Never set them down
Hey, I came in right on cue
One is me and one is you...
Hey, I came in right on cue
One is me and one is you...

from the album 'Heaven Up Here' 30/5/1981

SHROUD OF TURIN

I saw him
He saw me
That Turin-stained shroud
In Rimini
(He) cried
And I cried
We both died
Laughing
Him and me
Why me?
Why Rimini?

I want you
You want me
We both want
The things we'll never be now
We see now
It's sad how
Some things aren't meant to be
For we
Are just you and me

It never happens when you want it to
It never does what it's supposed to do
It's never good enough to see me through
See me through

I love that shroud that you're in
I love that you're maturing
I love that sweet sack you're in
I love your saccharin

It never happens when you want it to
It never does what it's supposed to do
It's never good enough to see me through
See me through

He saw me
I saw him
We both saw
Beneath each others'
Skin deep
Er than deep
We both sleep
To dream of what could be
For me
And sing hymns for him and me

I love that shroud that you're in
I love that you're from Turin

from the album 'The Fountain' 12/10/2009

SIBERIA

Where were we
Fearless and only ever scared of me
Peerless and tearless

  That was me
  Cold as ice
  On my knees
  Everynight
  Snow white

Where were you
When all the doors were closing
you forced me to
of all of us it´s you who chose

  Not me
  Cold as ice
  On my knees
  Everynight
  Snow white

Where were we
When I was fearless and only ever scared of me
Peerless and tearless

Where am I
Still trying to find the light
That burns the northern sky
A rarer borealis

Born to be
Made of lights
On my knees everynight
Snow bright

Yeh thats me
Cold as ice
On my knees
Everynight
Snow white

Born to be
Made of lights
On my knees everynight
Snow bright

from the album 'Siberia' 20/9/2005

SIDEWAYS EIGHT

It's us
Counting the one's we love
On the fingers of one glove
Collate
Count all the one's we hate
And side step the sideways eight

Move on, prove and improve on
You'll get your groove on and you'll get there
I'm sorry, baby don't worry
I'm just in a hurry to get somewhere

It's me
Still putting apostrophes
In every catastrophy
And it's you
Still making analogies
While I'm faking apologies

So move on, prove and improve on
You'll get your groove on and you'll get there
Sail on, hail and inhale on
Wagging your tail on
A different air

It's us
Counting the one's we love
On the fingers of one glove

So move on, prove and improve on
You'll get your groove on and you'll get there
Sail on, hail and inhale on
Wagging your tail on
A different air

Move on, prove and improve on
You'll get your groove on and you'll get there
I'm sorry, baby don't worry
I'm just in a hurry to get somewhere

I'm getting somewhere
am I getting somewhere
I'm sorry

from the album 'Siberia' 20/9/2005

SILVER

Swung from a chandelier
My planet sweet on a silver salver
Bailed out my worst fears
'Cos man has to be his own saviour
Blind sailors
Imprisoned jailers
God tamers
No one to blame us

The sky is blue
My hands untied
A world that's true
Through our clean eyes
Just look at you
With burning lips
You're living proof
At my fingertips

Walked on a tidal wave
Laughed in the face of a brand new day
Food for survival thought
Mapped out the place where I planned to stay
All the way
Well-behaved
Just in case it slips away

The sky is blue
My hands untied
A world that's true
Through our clean eyes
Just look at you
With burning lips
You're living proof
At my fingertips

from the album 'Ocean Rain' 8/5/1984

SIMPLE STUFF

We sat all night around a table
Trying to string three words together
Time has come and
By the way, mine's a double
By the way, mine's a double

Lucky for some
We don't understand
Everything we hear
We just pick out the simple stuff
Simple stuff
We don't need all those complications
We're tough stuff
And we got no intentions

b side from the single 'Rescue' 18/7/1980

SLIDELING

If you see me sliding
Say we're gonna slide together
If you see me hiding
Tell me I can hide forever

Come with me now
As now I run
Show me how to be someone
Let me fly into your sun

When my clouds are crying
Say your gonna change my weather
If you hear me lying
Its never when we lie together

Come with me now
As now I run
Show me how to be someone
Let me fly into your sun

If you see me sliding
Pray that I won't slide forever
If you see me hiding
Say that we can hide together

Come with me now
'Cos now I run
Show me how to be someone
Let me fly into your sun

Come with me now
'Cos now I run
Show me how to be someone
Let me fly into your sun

Your sun...

from the album 'Slideling' 28/4/2003

STAKE YOUR CLAIM

Stake your claim and take your touch
Make this pain not hurt so much

Come and save me, come and save me
Come and fix me up like new
Come and save me, come and save me
Do those tricks you used to do

I'll take my aim and place my bet
I know this game's not over yet
Know what I want now
Know what I want now
Know what I want now
Know what I want now

Come and save me, come and save me
Come and fix me up like new
Come and save me, come and save me
Do the tricks you used to do

Gotta be there when you get the call
Got to be the dust that falls from stars
Got to walk it like you know it all
Take the universe and make it our baby

And just maybe
And just maybe
You can fix me up like new
Come and save me, come and save me
Do the tricks you used to do

Don't be late
Don't waste a beat
I'll lick your plate, it tastes so sweet
I will I will I will I will

from the album 'Slideling' 28/4/2003

STARS ARE STARS

The sky seems full
When you're in the cradle
The rain will fall
And wash your dreams

Stars are stars
And they shine so hard

Now you spit out the sky
Because it's empty and hollow
All your dreams
Are hanging out to dry

Stars are stars
And they shine so cold

 I saw you climb
 Shadows on the trees
 We lost some time
 After things that never matter

I caught that falling star
It cut my hands to pieces
Where did I put that box
It had my name in it

 I saw you climb
 Shadows on the trees
 We lost some time
 After things that never matter

The cogs have clicked
And the clocks will have their
Say in the
Making of a day

You came here late
You've gone home early
Who'll remember now
You've gone away
Gone away, gone away

from the album 'Crocodiles' 18/7/1980

STORMY WEATHER

Hope you're feeling better now
Hope you got my letter, how
Is my stormy weather now?
Is she gonna change?

Can't we like everyone?
Pretending that there's nothing wrong?
Remember when we walked upon
clouds that never rained?

And I need it more than love
And I love it more than life
And I want those stars above to shine on this night

Have you ever wondered why?
I could make you laugh and cry?
Eclipsing all your summer skies
some things never change

And I need it more than love
And I love it more than life
And I want those stars above to shine this night

You want it?
You got it
There's nothing chained down
You need it?
I'll steal it
Just put your name down
I'll put my name down

Hope you're feeling better now
Hope you got my letter how
Is my stormy weather now
Is my stormy weather now

Can't we be like everyone?
Pretending that there's nothing wrong?
Remember when we walked upon
Remember when we walked upon
Remember when we walked upon
Remember when we walked upon
Clouds that never rained
But every cloud must rain

And I need it more than love
And I love it more than life
And I want those stars above to shine this night

You want it?
You've got it
There's nothing chained down
You need it?
I'll steal it
Just put your name down
I'll put my name down
You want it?
You've got it
Now I know it's to you I'm bound
You need it?
Godspeed it
Just put your name down
I'll put my name down

How's my stormy weather now?
How's the stormy weather now?
How's the stormy weather now?
How's my stormy weather now?
How's the stormy weather now?
How's my stormy weather now?

How's my stormy weather?

from the album 'Slidling' 28/4/2003

SUBWAY TRAIN

I looked in the eye of a hurricane
I was blown away
Another storm and another rain
On another day
I was Icarus's rings of fire
As I hit the ground
Meltdown city when I got too high
I'm never coming 'round

In my veins, in my veins
You're the subway and I'm the train

Choo-choo

b side from the single 'Never' 22/10/1995

SUPERMELLOWMAN

Will you walk through my storm
Can I be your one and only
Will you talk me through 'till dawn
Never felt so lost and lonely

When night turns into morning
And you don't know how long you must wait
As life came without warning
Your destiny will come too late

In the pool of my life
Kissing the ground that made me
Ancient rules wrong from right
Wish I'd found you when you could save me

When night turns into morning
And you don't know how long you must wait
As life came without warning
Your destiny will come too late

Can it ever be the same
Will we ever dream again
Walk through the sweet, sweet pain of love

No one ever broke the bough
The cradle fell anyhow
There's angels in the thunder clouds, above

When night turns into morning
And you don't know how long you must wait
As life came without warning
Your destiny will come too late

Kiss the ground...

from the album 'Flowers' 16/2/2001

THE BACK OF LOVE

I'm on the chopping block
Chopping off my stopping thought
Self doubt and selfism
Were the cheapest things I ever bought
When you say it's love
D'you mean the back of love
When you say it's love
D'you mean the back of love?

We're taking advantage of
Breaking the back of love
We're taken advantage of
Breaking the back of love

Easier said than done you said
But it's more difficult to say
With eyes bigger than our bellies
We want to but we can't look away
What were you thinking of
When you dreamt that up?
What were you thinking of
When you dreamt that up?

Taking advantage of
Breaking the back of love

When you're surrounded by a simple chain of events
Eventually you'll shack those shackles off

We can't tell our left from right
But we know we love extremes
Getting to grips with the ups and downs
Because there's nothing in between
When you say that's love

D'you mean the back of love
When you say that's love
D'you mean the back of love?

Taking advantage of
Breaking the back of love

What were you thinking of
When you dreamt that up?

We're taking advantage of
We're breaking the back of love
Breaking the back of love

from the album 'Porcupine' 4/2/1983

THE CAPE

All confused and all-consuming
Scaled the heights of dizzy love
Didn't know how vertigo
Could leave me in the balance of
My heart and all the gods above
Stung and all strung up

  It's only navigation
  So I'm moving overground
  Past the cape of levitation
  I'll keep hanging in when all the chips are down

Wooden houses, telegraph poles
Gave me reason and my shape
Casting shadows, marking pathways
Signposts showing our escape
Signposts showing our escape
The day, the time, the place

  It's only navigation
  So I'm moving overground
  Past the cape of all temptation
  I'll keep hanging in when all the chips are down

All aboard and all or nothing
All for one and one for all
The information must be hidden
Not not not for one and all
Not not not for one and all
One push and we will fall

  It's only navigation
  So I'm moving overground
  Past the cape of levitation
  I'll keep hanging in
  When all the chips are down

from the album 'Candleland' 17/9/1989

THE CUTTER

Who's on the seventh floor
Brewing alternatives
What's in the bottom drawer
Waiting for things to give

  Spare us the cutter
  Spare us the cutter
  Couldn't cut the mustard

Conquering myself until
I see another hurdle approaching
Say we can, say we will
Not just another drop in the ocean

Come to the free for all
With sellotape and knives
Some of us six feet tall
We will escape our lives

  Spare us the cutter
  Spare us the cutter
  Couldn't cut the mustard

Conquering myself until
I see another hurdle approaching
Say we can, say we will
Not just another drop in the ocean

Am I the happy loss
Will I still recoil
When the skin is lost
Am I the worthy cross
Will I still be soiled
When the dirt is off

Conquering myself until
I see another hurdle approaching
Say we can, say we will
Not just another drop in the ocean
Ocean

Watch the fingers close
When the hands are cold

Am I the happy loss
Will I still recoil
When the skin is lost
Am I the worthy cross
Will I still be soiled
When the dirt is off

Am I the happy loss
Will I still be soiled
When the dirt is off

from the album 'Porcupine' 4/2/1983

THE DEAD END

Is it real or imitation
Life, the big and black dead end
All these hand-me-down emotions
Just a mask to help pretend
That I'm gonna leave this station
A happy man among sad men

Take your chance
It's now or never
And then it's passed
Forever

Are you planning to remain
On the outside looking in
Well everything be all in vain
And all the chances be so slim
Sad to see you all still waiting
For your boat to come back in

Take your chance
It's now or never
And then it's passed
Forever
Hold this time
And capture it
And make your final wish

b side from the single 'Proud To Fall' 21/8/1989

THE DISEASE

My life's the disease
That could always change
With comparative ease
Just given the chance
My life is the earth
'Twixt muscle and spade
We wait for the worth
Digging for just one chance

As prospects diminish
As nightmares swell
Some pray for heaven
While we live in hell

My life's the disease
My life's the disease

If you get yours from heaven
Don't waste them
If you get yours from heaven
Don't waste them
If you get yours from heaven

from the album 'Heaven Up Here' 30/5/1981

THE FLICKERING WALL

In my world, my little world
Life lies upon the floor
The wind blows in and out again
Through windows and through doors
And it's there I'll look and it's there I'll find
What it was I started after
When I mistook what I had in mind
For something made to matter

   I heard the footsteps in the street
   I saw the lights on the flickering wall
   I moved my lips but I couldn't speak
   Choked on the wonder of it all
   Choked on the wonder
   Of it all

In my dreams, recurring dreams
But I was never there
Life so still invisible
Just needing to be where
With any luck I might just find
What it was I started after
When I undertook what I had in mind
When everything mattered

   When I saw the gods up in the sky
   I saw the lights on the flickering wall
   I saw the world through hazel eyes
   And choked on the wonder of it all
   Choked on the wonder
   Of it all...

from the album 'Candleland' 17/9/1989

THE FOUNTAIN

I slept by the mountain
Of rivers we crossed
I dreamt of the fountain
And the coin that we tossed

Now I'm just counting
The dreams that were lost
One coin in a fountain
Was all that it cost
Is that all it cost ?

I followed the oceans
I swallowed the seas
I buried emotions
I couldn't set free

I took every potion
From A to me
And that was devotion
Was that really me ?
Is that really me ?

 What a way to waste your wishes
 Changing something for somehow
 What I'd pay to taste your kisses, oh yeah
 Here and now, here and now, here and now
 D'you hear me now

Will there be thunder?
Will lightning strike?
Will I kneel in wonder
In a tunnel of light?

Will I go under?
And give up the fight
When they call my number
Called in the night
Call in the night

I cried the fountain dry
I climbed the mountains high
Hallelujah... hallelujah...
I got to you

from the album 'The Fountain' 12/10/2009

THE GAME

A sense of duty
Was my one intention
And an ugly beauty
Was my own invention
Pride a proud refusal
And I refuse
To need your approval
Too many seekers
Too few beacons
But through the fog
We'll keep on beaming

  Through the crying hours
  Of your glitter years
  All the living out
  Of your tinsel tears
  And the midnight trains
  I never made
  'Cos I'd already
  Played... the game

Everybody's
Got their own good reason
Why their favorite season
Is their favorite season
Winter winners
And those summers suns
Aren't good for everyone
Aren't good for everyone
Spring has sprung
And autumns so well done
So well done

And it's a better thing
That we do now
Forgetting everything
The whys and hows
While you reminisce
About the things you miss
You won't be ready
To kiss... goodbye

The earth is a world
The world is a ball
A ball in a game
With no rules at all
And just as I wonder
At the beauty of it all
You go and drop it
And it breaks when it falls

I'll never understand
Why you thought I would
Need to be reassured
And be understood
When I always knew
That your bad's my good
And I was ready
Ready... to be loved

Born under Mars
With Jupiter rising
Fallen from stars
That lit my horizon

I'll never understand
Why you thought I would
Need to be reassured
And be understood
When I always knew
That your bad's my good
And I was ready
Ready... to be

Through the crying hours
Of your glitter years
All the living out
Of your tinsel tears
And the midnight trains
I never made
'Cos I'd already
Played

It's a better thing
That we do now
Forgetting everything
The whys and hows
While you reminisce
About the things you miss
You won't be ready
To kiss... goodbye

from the album 'Echo & The Bunnymen' 6/7/1987

THE IDOLNESS OF GODS

If the world was half as mad as me
Like that could ever be
I'd say the world was crazy

If I'm just half the man I was
I'd say that's just because
I must have gotten lazy
Lazy...

  In duty and in love
  In beauty wearing off
  Beware, be wary of
  The Idolness of Gods

On the ropes against the tide
There's nowhere left to hide
Once you've seen my insides

Broken hope broke open wide
See the knock-out punch your pride
I've got you seats at ringside
Ringside...

  In duty and in love
  In beauty wearing off
  Beware, be wary of
  The Idolness of Gods

Oh, what now?
Oh, what now?
No, not now

Nights and tears are falling down
Keep splashing to the ground
Eyelashes getting drowned-drowned
Life's frontiers grew walls around
New pastures can't be found
I'm crashing cars in your town
Your town

In duty and in love
In beauty wearing off
Beware, be wary of
The Idolness of Gods

from the album 'The Fountain' 12/10/2009

THE KILLING MOON

Under blue moon I saw you
So soon you'll take me
Up in your arms
Too late to beg you
Or cancel it though I know it must be
The Killing Time...
Unwillingly mine

Fate
Up against your will
Through the thick and thin
He will wait until
You give yourself to him

In starlit nights I saw you
So cruelly you kissed me
Your lips a magic world
Your sky all hung with jewels
The Killing Moon
Will come too soon

Fate
Up against your will
Through the thick and thin
He will wait until
You give yourself to him

Under blue moon I saw you
So soon you'll take me
Up in your arms
Too late to beg you
Or cancel it though I know it must be
The Killing Time...
Unwillingly mine

Fate
Up against your will....

from the album 'Ocean Rain' 8/5/1984

THE PUPPET

I practice my fall
For practice makes perfect
Chained to the wall
For maximum hold
The window too far
Too far from my legs
Oh, open the door
And let out the cold

  You knew about this
  With your head in your hands
  All along
  I was the puppet, I was the puppet

Trampoline's broken
Ceiling has come down
The ache in my back
Tells me something's gone wrong
Rocking horse rocks
As the wallpaper peels
Curtain would like to know
What he has done

  You knew about this
  With your head in your hands
  All along
  I was the puppet, I was the puppet

We're the salt of the earth
And we know what to say
We're the salt of the earth
We know our place

  You knew about this
  With your head in your hands
  All along
  I was the puppet, I was the puppet

single release 14/9/1980

THE SUBJECT

You know exactly what is good for you
Bottle love and no dictionary
Shoving your face into anyone
Skating around the subject
With your skin undone
Rubbing your fingers into anyone

So far so good but what's good for me?

You know just exactly what is good for you
Bottle love and no dictionary
Tell me what you're thinking is good for me
Bottle love and no dictionary

Skating around the subject
Is my skin undone?
Mating with the subject
Subject, anyone?

b side from the single 'The Back Of Love' 14/1/1983

THE WHITE HOTEL

I want to be on that white-capped mountain peak
Above the lake, above my station
A moving carriage
The perfect marriage
Of life apart from destination

Ringing all the bells
Down at the white hotel
Tonight

I want to write the letters of persecution
To someone I don't know who doesn't know me
I want to be the dust inside a vacuum
An ice cube frozen in the melting sea

Ringing all the bells
Down at the white hotel
Ringing all the bells
Down at the white hotel
Tonight...

from the album 'Candleland' 17/9/1989

THE WORLD IS FLAT

Soul sucked and drowned
Woodchips on the sidings
Phased and dazed I found
My star was out and smiling
Life's song, and shining

You say you're gonna be someone
Ian's gonna make you smile
Still waiting for the day to come
'Til then you'll be a Wednesday's child

Opposites attract
Nothing's ever chosen
Gravity is fact
And every moment frozen
All gilded golden

You tell me that you know someone
Who says that you're his favorite girl
He's gonna give you all you want
'Cos all you want's his little world

 The World is flat...

I was in a dream
Where beauty dressed and killed
Saw babies born in boxes
And Jesus on a hill
And I felt evil

You said you know the world is flat
Nothings gonna change your mind
You know the only way is back
To gather what you've left behind

 The World is flat...
 For Wednesday's child

from the album 'Candleland' 17/9/1989

THE YO YO MAN

Froze to the bone in my igloo home
Counting the days 'til the ice turns green
You know when heaven and hell collide
There are no in-betweens

(I'm the yo-yo man)
Flames on your skin of snow turn cold
(Always up and down)
Cold is the wind that blows through my headstone

Collecting the bones of my friends tonight
Sowing the seeds in a fruitless land
You know when prayers all hit the ground
There is no higher hand

(I'm the yo-yo man)
Flames on your skin of snow turn cold
(Always up and down)
Cold is the wind that blows through my headstone
I'm the yo-yo man, always up and down
So take me to the end of your tether

(I'm the yo-yo man)
Flames on your skin of snow turn cold
(Always up and down)
Cold is the wind that blows through my...

(I'm the yo-yo man)
Flames on your skin of snow turn cold
(Always up and down)
Cold is the wind that blows through my...
(I'm the yo-yo man)
And the flames on your skin of snow turn cold
(Always up and down)
Cold is the wind that blows through our headstones

from the album 'Ocean Rain' 8/5/1984

THINK I NEED IT TOO

Must have forgotten something
How to forget how to be true
Covered myself in numb things
Don't touch me and I won't touch you

Trying to remember something
Why am I here ? and who are you ?
You must have meant something
When animals came in two by two

Whatever you want
Whatever you need
Whatever you want
Whatever you need
Think I need it too
I think I need it too
I think I need it too

Just as I thought I'm thinking
How can I change when I don't want to
Kept getting caught kept drinking
How can I blame what I've got to
Putting the wheels in motion
Auto-pilot, I can't drive
Covered in calomine lotion
Scratching my heatlumps bee-stung hives

Whatever you want
Whatever you need
Whatever you want
Whatever you need
Think I need it too
I think I need it too
I think I need it too

from the album 'The Fountain' 12/10/2009

THORN OF CROWNS

Ah ah, ah ah
Ah ah, ah ah

You set my teeth on edge
You set my teeth on edge
You think you're a vegetable
Never come out of the fridge

C-c-c-cucumber
C-c-c-cabbage
C-c-c-cauliflower
Men on Mars
April showers
Oh oh, oh oh

You are a dying breed
You are a dying breed
You once was an Inca
Now you're a Cherokee

C-c-c-cucumber
C-c-c-cabbage
C-c-c-cauliflower
Men on Mars
April showers

(You kick it, kick it)
(Ow uh, ow uh)
(Ow uh, ow uh, ow uh)

Wait for me on the blue horizon
Blue horizon for everyone
Wait for me on a new horizon
New horizons for everyone

I want to be one times one with you
Oh oh
I want to be one times one with you
Oh oh
Ah ah, ahh
Ah ah, ahh

I've decided to wear my thorn of crowns
I've decided to wear my thorn of crowns
Inside out
Back to front
Upside down
All the way round
Round, round round

I've decided to wear my thorn of crowns
I've decided to wear my thorn of crowns
Upside down
Inside out
Back to front
All the way round, down
Down, down, down, down
Down, down, down, down, down
Down, down, down, down, down
Down, down, down, down, down
Down, down, down, down, down

from the album 'Ocean Rain' 8/5/1984

TOAD

Feeling strange and unsure
In the place where I'm standing
Feeling stained and impure
And I'm frightened of landing
Tie a flag on my head
Take a walk on a moonbeam
Just forget what she said
She doesn't know what she means

Five fingers and four divisions
That was all I ever counted
Well provided with all provisions
That was all I ever wanted

No escape from the truth
No return from the deep
Just a failure in faith
And a hunch in a heap
Stop the light coming in
Tell the day not to break
Let the night draw me in
And the walls not to shake

Call out the fire engines
We're going down in a blaze of glory
Turn all the hosepipes on and
Bring in the hanging jury
Hang 'em high

We're cleaning the city now...

b side from the single 'Faith & Healing' 6/11/1989

TOO YOUNG TO KNEEL

Who's gonna hold you when you're too scared to feel?
Who's gonna cure you when the pain won't heal?
Who's gonna be there when your world goes wrong?
Who's gonna tell you you're the only one?

In my blood, in my soul
In this mind of mine
Can your touch turn me gold
Make my glitter shine

Who's gonna reach you when you can't be caught?
Who's gonna teach you what you can't be taught?
Who's gonna beat you when you won't be fought?
Who's gonna buy you when you can't be bought?

In my blood, in my soul
In this mind of mine
Can your touch turn me gold
Make my glitter shine

Who's gonna pray for you when you're too young to kneel?
Who's gonna fake it when it gets too real?
One more question answered in the falling stars
I heard they found
Death on Mars

from the album 'Evergreen' 14/7/1997

TURQUOISE DAYS

Just when the thought occurs
The panic will pass
And the smell of the fields
That never lasts
Put your faith
In those crimson nights
Set sail
In those turquoise days

  You've got a problem
  Come on over
  You've got a problem
  Come on over

It's not for glory
It's not for honour
Just something someone said
It's not for love
It's not for war
Just hands clasped together

It's not for living
It's not for hunger
Just lips locked tight
It's not rebellion
It's not suffering
It's just the way it is

And my pistol's packed
And my God goes with me
I feel easy
And I want it
And I need it
And I've got it

It's not for this
It's not for that
It's not any of it

Did you say knowledge?
Did you say prayer?
Did you say anything?
If not for good
If not for better
If not the way it is

Just when the thought occurs
The panic will pass
And the smell of the fields
Never lasts
We'll put your faith
In those crimson nights
Set sail
In those turquoise days

Place our faith
In those crimson nights
Set sail
In those turquoise days

You've got a problem
Come on over
You've got a problem
Come on over
Now I think I know
Just what to say
Now I think I know
Just what to say

from the album 'Heaven Up Here' 30/5/1981

VIBOR BLUE

Jigsaw man where have you gone?
Melted into morning
Don't believe and don't belong
Death-defying dawnings

Vibor blue
The have-nots and the have-to's
The frozen chosen few
Destined to see it through
Born to vibor blue

Estoy candalabarar
Obligoing brightly
Voy e vamos a las stars
Twice nightly never lightly

Vibor blue
The have-nots and the have, too
The frozen chosen few
Are here to take us through
Gateway vibor blue

Limitless forsoothiay
Yo tengo muchos nada
Vaya con Dias all the way
Me madness made me sadder
Estoy candelabarar
Obligoing brightly
Voy e vamos a las stars
Twice nightly never lightly

Vibor blue
The have-nots and the have-to's
The frozen chosen few
Are here to take us, too
Born to vibor blue
Destined to see it through
Born to vibor blue

from the album 'Mysterio' 17/3/1992

VILLIERS TERRACE

I've been up to Villiers Terrace
To see what's happening
There's people rolling 'round on the carpet
Mixing up the medicine

I've been up to Villiers Terrace
To see what's happening

People rolling 'round on the carpet
Biting wool and pulling string
You said people rolled on carpet
But I never thought they'd do those things

I've been up to Villiers Terrace
I've been in a daze for days
I drank some of the medici-i-i-ine
And I didn't like the taste

I've been up to Villiers Terrace
I've been in a daze for days

People rolling 'round on your carpet
Biting wool and pulling string
You said people rolled on carpet
But I never thought they'd do those things

Been up to Villiers Terrace
To see what's happening
There's people rolling 'round on the carpet
Passing 'round the medicine

Been up to Villiers Terrace
To see what's happening

 There's people rolling 'round on my carpet
 Biting wool and pulling string
 You said people rolled on carpet, boys
 But I never thought they'd do those things

Bopsie waddy waddy
Shake your money
(Been down to Villiers Terrace)...
Bopsie waddy waddy
Shake your money
(Been down to Villiers Terrace)...
Bopsie waddy waddy
Shake your money
(Been down to Villiers Terrace)...
Bopsie waddy waddy
Save your money
(Been down to Villiers Terrace)...

from the album 'Crocodiles' 18/7/1980

WAY OUT AND UP WE GO

When I asked for money
You would give me alcohol
Wasn't being funny
When I said no ifs at all

I'm thinking thoughts too late
No linking
I won't wait

When I wanted coffee
You insist on alcohol
When I said no maybes
You would give me ifs, that's all

A message wrapped in paper
Each passage wrapped in paper
Wrapped in paper made for us
Wrapped in paper made for us

Some meaning sent to someone
Each read it, passed it on
Passed it on to one of us
Passed it on to one of us

Crumpled on the mattress
Best you cover up
Hardly in the bad day
When you don't get up

He made it
Wrapped in sackcloth
Afraid of it
Had to back off
Backed off into one of us
Backed off into one of us

Ten seconds
You can't see it
Old record
Laugh my way out

Way out and up we go
Out of the way and up we go

b side from the single 'The Cutter' 14/1/1983

WEBBED

Up above me
And inside me
All around me and you
Are no victims
And no victories
Just the guilty few

Hey
Here comes my world
And hey
Here comes my real world

Stalking dreams
Through wind and rain
I've sold my heart and soul again

In the window
There's a shadow
Someone borrowed from me
There's a sunset
Low and lonely
On an island
At sea

Hey
Is this my world?
And hey
Is this my real world?

Stalking dreams
Through wind and rain
I've sold my heart and soul again

Up above me
And inside me
All around me
Something aching
Something breaking
Something shaking
In me

Hey
Here comes our world
And hey
There goes my real
Real world

from the album 'Mysterio' 17/3/1992

WHAT ARE YOU GOING TO DO WITH YOUR LIFE?

If I knew now what I knew then
I'd wonder how not wonder when
There's something going wrong again
With me and mine
It's only ever what it seems
Memories and might have beens
Heaven's scent: the smell of dreams
We'll never find

Tell me, tell me, tell me

  What are you going to do with your life?
  What are you going to do with your life?
  What are you going to do?
  What are you going to be?
  What am I going to do?
  I'm going to be me, be me, be me

If I could see what you can see
The sun still shining out of me
I'd be the boy I used to be
When love was blind
I'd let the light back in again
Walk you to the tunnel's end
I'd be yours and maybe then
You'd be mine

So tell me, tell me, tell me
What are you going to do with your life?...

I will, if you will
Follow me down...

from the album 'What Are You Going To Do With Your Life?' 16/4/1999

WHAT IF WE ARE?

Maybe you're not the world
Maybe you're not the stars
Maybe you're not the girl
What if you are?

Maybe I'm not the boy
Maybe I'm not the man
Maybe I'm not the one
But what if I am?
Yeah, what if I am?

 Then it's love, yes, it's love like it could be
 It's love yes, yes, it's love like it should be

Maybe the dream
Is only a wish
Not what it seems
So what if it is?
Maybe it doesn't fly
On the wings of a dove
Maybe it's just the life
What if it's love?
Yeah, what if it's love?

 Then it's love, yes, it's love, like it could be
 It's love yes, yes, it's love, like it should be
 Is it love? Yes, it's love, like it could be
 It's love, yes, it's love, like it should be

'Cause I know I'm alive
'Cause I know I'm not dead
And I know I'm alive
'Cause I know I'm not dead

I know what's going down
I know what's going down
I know what's coming down
I know I'm coming down

Hey, have I hit rock bottom?
And hey, how to hit rock bottom
Maybe you're not the world
Maybe you're not the stars
Maybe you're not the girl,
What if you are?

Maybe I'm not the boy,
Maybe I'm not the man
Maybe I'm not the one,
What if I am?
Yeah, what if I am?

Then it's love, yes, it's love, like it could be
It's love, yes, it's love, like it should be
Is it love? Yes, it's love, like it could be
Love, yes, it's love, like it should be

'Cause I know I'm alive
'Cause I know I'm not dead
It's love, yes, it's love like it could be
Love, yes, it's love, like it should be
Is it love? Yes, it's love, like it could be
Love, yes, it's love, like it should be
I'm not dead

Hey, have I hit rock bottom?
Have I hit rock bottom?
Tell me, hey, how to hit rock bottom?
How to hit rock bottom...

from the album 'Siberia' 20/9/2005

WHEN IT ALL BLOWS OVER

When it all blows over
Can we start again?
When we've both grown older
Will you love me then?
Say you'll love me then

You never had to tell me
I already knew
The first time you held me
It was only you
It was only ever you

Through every change
As I turned with the tide
Through all of my games
You were there by my side

When it all blows over
Can we start again?
When we've both grown older
Will you love me then?
Say you'll love me then

Will you love me then?
Say you'll love me then?
Did you love me then...?

from the album 'What Are You Going To Do With Your Life?' 16/4/1999

WITH A HIP

Halt halt halt halt
Nobody's allowed
Strictly verboten
Out out out out
Bounds, of course we know no bounds
Until, at least, and then
We trespass all the way down

They've got it and I want some
I can handle it, and I want some
Relax, feel the pleasure inside
Error and trial, collide collide

You won't listen
I don't expect you to
We've lost
And something's all we can do

With a hip hip hop and a flip flap flop
Gonna steal some bananas from the grocer's shop
With your head in the clouds
And your trousers undone
Gonna shit on the carpet
Just like everyone

This is the one for the money
This is the one for the trees
This is the one called heaven
And this is the one for me

You've yet to discover
Discover the difference
The difference between the moral and motto
They've got it and I had some
I couldn't handle it but I had some

Hold it in the light
And see right through it
For god's sake make a decision
Take it for a walk
And hold it hold it
Pin it on the wall and fasten onto

Move into the bathroom
Oh yes oh yes
Do what must be done
And don't say maybe

This is the one for the money
This is the one for the trees
This is the one called heaven
And this is the one for me

from the album 'Heaven Up Here' 30/5/1981

ZEPHYR

Can you be the one
To help me understand myself?
The one and only one
Is it you and no-one else?
Can you shoot for things
That others only dream about?
Can you light the fire
When all my flames are dying out?

Can you be the one...
To tell me about my life
Tell me about my world
Tell me about your life
Tell me about your world

Don't look to the crowd
Aim above and out beyond
Leave the common ground
You never wanted to belong
The sky is open wide
Light the fuse and take a ride
Leave it all behind
Dig in deep and push aside

You know you're the one...
Tell me about my life
Tell me about my world
Tell me about your life
Tell me about your world

Shoot them down
They wanna drag you down
Got to see
They're your enemies...

Listen you can't even see
What this world has done to me
Done to me...

from the album 'Burned' 1/10/1995